LIFE IS FOR LAUGHING AT

with warmest regards

Gordon

GORDON FARQUHAR   *December 2005*

Published 2005 by arima publishing

www.arimapublishing.com

ISBN 1-84549-059-2

Printed and bound in the United Kingdom

Typeset in Garamond 10/14

swirl is an imprint of arima publishing

arima publishing
ASK House, Northgate Avenue
Bury St Edmunds, Suffolk IP32 6BB
t: (+44) 01284 700321

www.arimapublishing.com

This book is dedicated to the memory of my Dear Father from whom I could have learned so much if only I had possessed the patience to listen to him more often than I did.

CONTENTS

INTRODUCTION

Not everyone has a similar sense of humour and certainly, of those people who might just happen to pick up this book, not everyone will share mine!

I tend to like attempts to bring fun out of everyday aspects of life – without being cruel or sadistic. There are many happenings on most days which really just cry out 'laugh at me' or 'twist me around, add a touch of imagination and *then* laugh at me'! I have tried, from time to time, to spot potential ideas, based on this premise, and to develop them. Such items form the basis for most of this book.

Furthermore, however, I have always enjoyed a wide variety of different forms of humour. I enjoy poems and jokes, and over the years I have jotted down items which, at the time, made *me* laugh. Good after-dinner speeches can, of course, be a source of much fun but how often does one hear 'I heard some great stories but I never seem to remember them later'? I too am like that, so I have, on occasion, noted a few key words which have let me reconstruct a joke at a later time – or perhaps I hoped that I might even improve upon the original!

I have, over the years, collected many pieces of paper containing funny stories, jokes, and other items of interest. My Father, who always seemed to have a play or a pantomime in his typewriter, started off my collection by leaving me his own 'little book of gems'.

As I said above, I have always been able to appreciate a variety of different types of humour. So, in setting down this, my collection of humour, I have deliberately mixed up the dates and the types – nothing being more boring to me than to read 'jokes in categories'. In addition, however, I have included a few non-funny but interesting items which, I hope, will give a balance in my miscellaneous collection.

Naturally, I have many people to thank for my material. However, the sources of my jokes, and even of some basic ideas on which I may have written, are many, varied and long since forgotten. In the 'jokes business' it is difficult to be entirely original, so one cannot be sure whose work is whose: suffice to say that one person feeds off another, hopefully even 'adding value' to someone else's ideas. If I have made any glaring omissions of thanks I hope I may be forgiven.

In conclusion, may I reiterate that I do firmly believe, as the chosen title states, that everyday life can be made much more enjoyable if one can find something in it to laugh at. Laughter can indeed often be the best medicine for many ailments.

7 December, 2004

My Dear Daughter

After being retired for 9 Years I received, rather unexpectedly, a nice letter from a company called Job-serve. They very thoughtfully asked if I was satisfied with my current employment and implied that, if I was not, they might be able to place me elsewhere. Without even consulting you or my present employer – your Mother – I rejected their offer. I have to say that I worried that 'the placement' might be into a Home for the Mentally Disturbed! For your information I attach a copy of my Letter. Perhaps you will think that I was a little hasty?

I realise that you must often wonder what I do with all the so called 'spare time' I gained upon retiring from my engineering career. Perhaps the following collection of letters and other assorted papers will partially assist you with your puzzlement.

Over the years I have collected - having scribbled on various pieces of papers - a miscellany of jokes and other humorous items, not all of them written by me I hasten to add. I felt compelled to tidy 'the heap' and to type some of them into a more easily read format. As you know, I have also, from time to time, written some letters in which I have endeavoured to offer a little praise, a little chastisement or even a touch of 'Micky Taking' to certain colleagues and friends. I am sending herewith a selection for your perusal.

Just one more thing, you will see the references in some of these masterpieces of English literature to a *Lord Farquhar of Hatfield*; it will not be difficult for someone of your intelligence to work out that I am indeed that 'Nobleman'. I am truly sorry that you are discovering for the first time that you have aristocratic blood in your veins. Please put this down to my inbred modesty – I hope you are not terribly embarrassed.

I hope you get some enjoyment from reading these witterings of an old fool………

Your ever loving Father

* * * * * * * *

Senility House
70 Andover Street
Kilmacolm

30 August, 2001

The Managing Director
Job-serve Limited

Dear Madam

Recruitment for Executive Positions

Thank you for your recent letter in which you posed the questions 'Are you fully appreciated in your existing job?' and 'Does your current position offer you the opportunity to fulfil your potential?'

I have to answer both questions in the negative.

I gave up Structural Engineering in 1992, since when I have tried my hand at a wide variety of rather dull occupations. These have included gardening, washing windows, unblocking kitchen sinks, etc.. Whilst the financial rewards have not been high, I think I *am* appreciated by the mistress of the house who has allowed me to sleep with her from time to time.

I did contemplate becoming a golf professional - a game at which I have excelled on occasions; for example, I have had several holes in 2. I have kept my equipment up to date – carbon fibres, titanium, Wee Berthas, WD40, etc. I swing from right to left – rather like my politics. I do look after myself – I take a laxative tablet every night, a factor I feel contributed to my having a good run in a recent competition. I have, however, been singularly unfortunate with injuries; I have weaknesses in my back, my arms, my legs and my heart - as well as which I can't putt straight.

For several years I have been a member of a local Seniors Golf Team – a bunch of has-beens and cripples who don't win many matches. Although, through bad luck, I myself have lost the occasional game, it really is frustrating to be let down by others. My team mates talk of me as 'a big shot' (at least I think that's the word they use) so I have been asked to Captain the team tomorrow. However, since the team has recently had more leaders than the Conservative Party, I don't expect to keep *that* job for long.

You will gather that I am certainly not fulfilling my potential at present. Perhaps you can suggest what I should do.

Yours sincerely

Ivan Oldbody

* * * * * * * *

THE UNIVERSITY OF NORTH GREENOCK

Department of Adding and Subtracting

Dr. J R Santos
Secretariate Tolerencia
Department Matematico
Instituto Superiore Tecnico
MADRID, SPAIN

29 November 2003

Dear Dr. Santa

International Conference on Accuracy Estimates and Adaptive Refinements in Finite Element Computations

We refer to your 'call for papers' for the above Conference to be held in Lisbon on 19-22 June 2004.

We are a little unsure of the degrees of accuracy with which your Conference will deal. We ourselves consider that, for most local government financial analyses in the UK with which we assist, if we get anywhere near to plus or minus 85.83% we are doing rather well. However, I do know that, for the projects of certain Spanish Architects, such accuracy would be considered exceptionally good!

If we have interpreted your requirements correctly we would like to put forward our Mr. Jan Galileo Wilton who could present a paper entitled "Tolerance – why the wives of Local Government Officers need a lot".

Mr. Wilton will be well known to you, I am sure, as an expert in the use of finite element methods in the analysis of politicians' expenses. You may recall that he presented a paper on this subject last year at your PIG Conference (Polytecnico Instituto Granada). He has the additional qualifications, essential for a conference such as yours, that he knows how to get to Portugal and he hopes to obtain in the near future an 'O' level in arithmetic.

Yours faithfully

Professor G Whizz

Hon. Rector

Lord Farquhar of Hatfield

c. J G Wilton

3

SURVIVING A TOURING HOLIDAY

This is the tale of a Cosmos Tour;
They give you value – that's for sure!
The sights and stories all abound,
But your feet may never touch the ground.

It has to start with Leader Clint,
Who leads you off, with never a hint
Of historical landmarks you will find,
And statistics designed to blow your mind.

Savannah comes – Atlanta goes;
Did we see Memphis? God alone knows!

The miles rush past. You want to dose,
Eyelids are heavy – they want to close.
When up pops Clinton, smile on face,
Another part of *that war* to trace.

A beautiful story – he loves to prattle -
Another General ; another battle.
Dates and times are a terrible mix;
Was it 1830 – or half past six?
We're all confused – "Who won Tennessee?
Was it General Grant or Elvis P?"

Competitions cut you down to size ;
"Can you draw a cow – for a fabulous prize?"

Just when you thought 'Tonight I'll sleep',
Clinton's agile mind digs deep.
Your head – it aches; your feet are sore;
But it's "Cases out at half past four"!

If you survive, they write your name
In the Cosmos Travel Hall of Fame.

And, as you leave to board your plane –
To Home, and a chance to rest your brain;
You think – "Next year, will I go abroad?
A Cosmos Tour?"   Oh.....My.....God!

GFF   November 1995
Great South Tour (USA)

4

SURVIVING A CHANGING WORLD

(For Those Born Before 1940......)

We were born before television, penicillin, polio shots, frozen foods, Xerox, contact lenses, videos and The Pill. We were ahead of radar, credit cards, split atoms, laser beams and ball-point pens; before dishwashers, tumble driers, electric blankets, air conditioners, drip-dry clothes....and before a man walked on the moon.

We got married first and *then* lived together. We thought 'fast food' was what you ate during Lent; a 'Big Mac' was an oversized raincoat and 'crumpet' was what you had for tea. We existed before house-husbands, computer dating and we knew 'sheltered accommodation' as the place where you waited for a bus.

We were born before day care centres, group homes and disposable nappies. We never heard of FM radio, tape decks, DVDs, artificial hearts and word processors, nor did we see young men wearing earrings. For us, 'time sharing' meant togetherness, a 'chip' was a piece of wood or a fried potato, 'hardware' meant nuts and bolts and 'software' wasn't even a word.

Before 1940 'made in Japan' signified junk; the term 'making out' referred to how you did in your exams; a 'stud' was something that fastened a collar to a shirt and 'going all the way' meant staying on a tram-car to the terminus. In our day, cigarette smoking was fashionable, 'grass' was mown, 'coke' was kept in the coalhouse, a 'joint' was a piece of meat you ate on Sundays and 'pot' was something you cooked in. 'Rock music' was a fond mother's lullaby, cleavage was something the butcher did, a 'gay person' was the life and soul of the party, while 'aids' just meant beauty treatment or help for someone in trouble.

We who were born before 1940 must be a hardy bunch - if you just think of the way in which the world has changed and of the adjustments *we* have had to make. It is little wonder that there is a generation gap today.......BUT

By the Grace of God.....we have Survived!

Anon.

* * * * * * * *

5

GAGA HOLIDAYS plc

James Trowser Esq.
Beltit Road
KILMACOLM

SENILITY HOUSE
70 ANDOVER STREET
OLDHAM

1 February, 2004

Dear Mr. Trowser

The Director of Age Concern has kindly brought your name to my attention on the occasion of your having yet another Birthday. Congratulations on your becoming very elderly.

I realise that some people become quite distressed when they pass on (if I may use that phrase in the circumstances) into that social class known loosely as The Very Elderly. For this reason I would like to introduce the GAGA Group to you. We are a sister company to SAGA which, as you will know, looks after the needs of the over 50's; we also own FAGA which looks after those who continue to smoke, SHAGA which caters for the promiscuous of all ages and, of course, if you should wish to visit Australia you should contact WAGA-WAGA.

Membership of GAGA – which is open only to selected people of your seniority – brings a world of benefits. For example, our latest attractions include a one way ticket for a cheap climbing holiday on Mount Everest, or a 32 day trip to watch the Scotland cricket team playing in the next World Cup (and you may even be asked to play). GAGA also offer merchandising bargains such as trampolines, trendy thongs and therapeuticthingammies. Our Service Department can pursue your cold weather payments and we often arrange insurance cover, on advantageous terms, for those who have long since forgotten what they own.

I was very sorry to learn that your employment pension as a former teacher is no longer adequate for your needs – things can be very difficult under a Labour Government. We could perhaps arrange a re-training course to allow you to get a well paid job as an English translator at the new Scottish Parliament.

Well, what do you do next? There are no long complicated forms to fill up – simply send your cheque for £199 to me. I will then, if I remember, send you a membership card and, provided you apply within 7 days, your lucky Mystic Meg charm bracelet.

So remember, Mr Trowser, "when you become very elderly, you too can go GAGA".

Yours sincerely

Ivan Oldbody

Patron ; The Lord Farquhar of Hatfield

MEMO from - Kandi the Lovely Beagle

KILMACOLM KENNELS

23 July, 1974

Dear Adopted Grandmother,

I thought I would drop you a line to express my gratitude for the wonderful dog biscuits which you left for me on Thursday. I have never seen any quite so big; probably because my owners are so mean that they always buy the ordinary kind. Frankly, I do get fed up with them – one bite and they are gone.

I had a lot of enjoyment trying to eat through these 'Super Chews'. It was hard going, but I did eventually work out a technique. In any event, you know that I have a lot of patience for dealing with food of any kind. I have managed to save a few for later but have taken the precaution of hiding them – as you know, my Master has been known to pinch my biscuits from time to time.

We have had some lovely workmen around the house recently. They are adding another bedroom and thus making my kennel a little larger. They often forget to shut the gate, so I have been able to run away quite often. I can then have a wonderful time emptying the neighbours' bins – its amazing what an enterprising beagle can find! I always go home, of course, for my regular meals but it is fun sometimes to wait and make my Master come looking for me. I wish he would agree to give me 6 meals a day now that I am fully grown.

I have missed you very much since you went away. Apart from the special biscuits, I did enjoy the apple cores and other titbits you used to drop on the floor for me.

I think you're a lovely person and just wish your son, my Master, was as generous.

Thanks again

Much love

* * * * * * * *

"WHO WON THE BLOODY WAR ANYWAY?"

The Germans and the Japanese are very much the same –
Their schoolboys don't play rugger and cricket's not their game.
They don't tip caps to ladies; their manners are uncouth;
The Gorbal's gangs were angels – compared with Hitler's Youth.

>   So - We don't like the Germans and we hate the Japs;
>   They kick and shove and bully – they're simply rotten chaps.

We fought on corned beef fritters; we always dressed in style;
They ate raw fish and saur kraut and reeked at half a mile.
Their languages are funny – you often hear them sing
"Deutchland Uber Alles" and "Ying Tong Ying Tong Ying".

>   Yes - We don't like the Nippos; we can't stand the Krauts;
>   They aren't really like us – we'll always have our doubts.

We fought them on the beaches, we fought them in the street,
We fought them going forward, we fought them in retreat.
In peacetime our performance leaves us crying in our mince,
'Cos our workforce has been going back and forwards ever since.

>   But - They got cash for losing – "What *did* we do that for?"
>   It's left us asking questions like – "Who won the Bloody War?"

The Spaniards take our fish away, The Ities always cheat;
The Froggies smell of garlic and the Dutch won't buy our meat:
The Maastricht Treaty sank us – and the Aussies don't like Liz –
We haven't any friends at all, with whom to do our Biz'.

>   So --- We love Nippon exports – your Yen is quite unique;
>   We all love German motor cars – "Vorsprung Durch Technik".

GFF   VE Day + 50   May 1995

(Sung as a song at the Hatfield Court Street Party)

* * * * * * *

The Ministry of Wurks and Teknical Information

Whitehall   London

Engineering Drawings for the Ministry --- Guidance Notes

1. Before using pens ensure that they have ink in them.

2   All lines to be drawn should be straight, unless they have to be curved; in this case they should not be straight.

3

4   Drawings should be kept free of coffee stains, bird droppings and the like.

5. All spelling should be checked against the Oxford Dixshonary.

4. When prints of drawings require to be coloured please note that the Race Relations Board has decreed that black, orange, green, yellow and Chinese white should not be used.

5. Fag ends should not be stubbed out on drawings.

6. When working on projects with a high security classification, draughtsmen must wear blindfolds. Alternatively, invisible ink may be used.

7. Do not use 4 letter words on drawings – preferably use no more than 3 letters so that the supervising officer has a sporting chance of understanding your work.

8. Further assistance with this difficult subject can be obtained by reading one of the following publications;
    "Drawing Simplified" by L da Vinci
    "Teach Yourself Draughtsmanship" by D I Urselph
    "Feeling the Draught" by Gordon Brown

9. Information of a more confidential nature can be obtained by completing Form MI5/Psst.

Official Health Warning: Working for the Government can seriously damage your Sanity

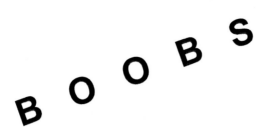

BOOBS

50 Kaye Walk
The Pier
BALFRON

22 May, 2003

Mrs. Lizzie Rosswell
Strathbuchan House
NEARBY

Dear Mrs. Rosswell

I write to you on behalf of the **B**ritish **O**lympic **O**rganising **B**ody for **S**cotland which intends to put in a bid to hold the Olympic Games in Scotland in 2012. We are seeking to counter President Blair's London bid and indeed, with good Scottish prudence, to put on a spectacular show at a fraction of the cost.

My Organisation is approaching you for your assistance. I should say at this stage that your name sprang to mind when I heard of your remarkable run in the recent Glasgow 10 km race where, I understand, you came within an hour of the world record for that distance.

We have in mind to put together a programme of novelty events which, by their simplicity, will appeal to Scots everywhere and which would be very economical. We would obviously include - for the first time in any Olympics - our unique national events like 'wellie boot throwing' and the 'haggis and spoon race'. However, under the general title of BONES (British Olympic Novelty Events in Scotland), we need lots of ideas. That is where you would come in! We would like you to head a special Committee of BOOBS to push forward women's main attributes.

The ability to market our objectives and bring in huge dollops of sponsorship money is important and, between you and me, I certainly intend to siphon off some of it for myself. We might have a wee Jack Russell as a mascot; this might also enable us to use the slogan 'Give the dog a BONE'.

When you have had time to consider this appointment please send a full CV elaborating, of course, on further examples of your athletic prowess and perhaps your ability at lateral thinking.

Yours sincerely

Directors
Lord Farquhar of Hatfield
Jackie Burd
Roland Bacon
Cathie Jamieson
Rod Stewart

Strathbuchan House, Nearly Nearby

Lord Farquhar of Hatfield
Kilmacolm

29 May 2003

My Lord

I hope you will forgive my writing to you directly rather than through your tasteful secretary Mr. Bacon. I just wanted to let you know how grateful I am for your uplifting news. At last my well endowed friends and I can look forward to BOOBS in all shapes and sizes for everyone!

Sadly, I have to advise you that I will have to decline your offer of candidacy for your fine organisation, on the grounds that, by an accident of birth, I am English! Furthermore, I am at this time very, very busy, given that I am currently CEO of the National English Reputable Drama Society (NERDS), an organisation which specialises in making a huge drama out of utter trivia. I am also at the forefront of pushing forward women's main attributes (as you so aptly put it) in several other areas. Two of these are the National Association of Fearless Females (NAFF) and the Professional Organisation of Oratory Personnel (POOPS). The latter is closely linked to POOFS (the Professional Organisation for Oratory Female Staff).

However, may I say that I have had a positive flood of fine ideas for the major cultural event that BOOBS is proposing. May I suggest that you could include some culinary activities such as throwing the scotch pie or guessing how much grease and how many calories are in a scotch pie. Other activities, involving Recipes with the Scottish staple diet of Irn Bru plus Salt & Vinegar crisps, could be even more exciting, particularly if given a blue and green theme, to encourage religious tolerance throughout the world.

In the meantime, I do thank you wholeheartedly for considering me for such an important post. Naturally, if you do manage to siphon off any spare cash from the proceedings then please do remember that I did at least reply to your offer; I also managed, by virtue of my supreme lateral thinking skills, to work out your home address.

With many, many thanks

Yours for ever
Lizzie Rosswell

MICHAEL FRANK BANNER FARQUHAR

Born - 16th July 1964

Preface to a commemorative Photo Album

Michael ---- A Father's Recollections

The story starts in Sixty Four -
A normal July morning;
An expectant hush hung in Laggan Road -
The Farquhars had given due warning.

The rain was pouring down, of course,
It was the Glasgow Fair;
The girls were told to be very quiet,
'Things are happening up the stair'.

The Doctor and the Midwife came,
They told me not to worry;
It all takes time – as the advert said
'You cannot hurry a Murray'.

'It's a boy' they cried, with shouts of glee
(we hadn't been able to guess):
'*We'll* cut the cord and hose him down,
While *you* clean up the mess'.

We photographed young Michael then;
We've done so ever since.
I've collected here a few of them;
Warning – some will make you wince!

GFF 2004

* * * * * * * *

A COLLECTION of JOKES

Blind Freefall Parachutist being interviewed: 'Do you judge when you are near the ground by changes in air pressure?' 'No; I wait until my guide dog's lead goes slack!'

The essence of surprise: 'You're *what*?' – as Joseph said to Mary.

Clairvoyant's Notice: 'The show has had to be cancelled due to unforeseen circumstances.'

'Dee-lightful': as the big negro said when he p...d into the chandelier.

The newest Irish West End Production – on the life of George Best.......... 'Liver Dance'.

Gerhard Schroder – Chancellor of Germany: He tried to create an impression as an orator by copying the style of John F Kennedy who, in Berlin, had said "Ich bin ein Berliner". So, on a visit to China, Schroder said "Ich bin ein Pekinese". Next week he goes to Hamburg!

Patience/stupidity; 'He was well through his 2000 piece jigsaw, when he discovered he had opened a packet of cornflakes'.

'I haven't spoken to my wife for three days' – 'I didn't want to interrupt'.

Husband arrives home at 4am; his wife is very angry. He explains that he met a beautiful but lonely actress visiting their home town; 'It would have been impolite to leave her on her own, so I took her a) for a meal; b) to her hotel in a taxi; c) upstairs to her room'. His angry wife retorted 'a likely story – you've been out playing poker with your pals'.

Scot; 'I've bought a lovely mink muff for my wife, tae keep her hands warm'. English friend; 'What fur?'. Scot; 'I've jist telt ye'.

For sale; Electric car, only £2 – plus £2000 for the flex.

Scot to Irishman at bottom of hole; 'Did you fall down there? Irishman; 'No, down *here*'.

'I got wonderful pills to give me strength'; 'Did they work?'; 'I don't know – I can't get the top off the bottle'.

Doctor, at medical strip examination; 'How long has it been like that?'. Patient; 'That's as long as it has ever been'.

Joe said to me that he's making a comeback. Personally, I'm not aware that he has ever been anywhere significant'.

To Prince Charles (about his 50th birthday party); 'Did you have all your usual favourites – Jammie Dodgers, soft sponges and nutty fruit cake?'. 'Yes, the whole family was there'.

"OH, THOSE SCOTS"

Nowhere can an Englishman turn to escape Scottish ingenuity.

He goes to work in a raincoat patented by chemist Charles Macintosh;
He strides along a lane surfaced by John Macadam;
He drives a car fitted with tyres invented by John Boyd Dunlop;
At work, he receives mail bearing adhesive stamps invented by James Chalmers;
He uses the telephone – an invention of Alexander Graham Bell.

At home, his child rides a bicycle invented by Kirkpatrick Macmillan;
He watches the news on television – an invention of John Logie Baird;
He hears an item about the U S Navy – founded by John Paul Jones.

In desperation, he picks up the Holy Bible – only to find that King James V1
    of Scotland authorised its translation;
He would like a drink – but the Scots make the world's best whisky;
He could end it all with a breech loading rifle invented by Captain Patrick Ferguson;
But, if he survives and undergoes surgery, he may be given penicillin –
    co-discovered by Sir Alexander Fleming;
Coming out of the anaesthetic, discovered by Sir James Young Simpson,
He would find no comfort in thinking he was 'as safe as the Bank of England' –
    it was founded by William Paterson.

Perhaps his only remaining hope would be a transfusion of *guid* Scottish blood,
    which would entitle him to ask----'*Wha's like us?*'

Anon.

* * * * * * * *

14

A HEROIC RESCUE

I could see the fellow waving – as I walked along the shore,
His cries of "Help me, Help me" I couldn't quite ignore.

I shouted "Wait a minute – I can't come in quite yet,
I've got my Sunday suit on and I mustn't get it wet".

"Can't you see that I am drowning; Save me" came the cry
"If you don't dive in and help me, I am surely going to die".

I folded my clothes by the lakeside, my shoes were laid carefully by;
I was ready to jump in the water, when I thought of my shirt and my tie.

The water was pleasantly warm, as I swam my way out from the shore;
There was peace, and a stillness, around me, 'cos the decibel level was lower.

He was moaning, but lacking in small talk, when I pulled him right back to the edge;
It was pleasing to see, as I noted with glee, that my clothes were still there on the ledge.

I threw him on to his backside, and my hands pumped away at his chest;
I battled on for a long time 'though I badly needed a rest.

His mouth kept spewing out water, and sometimes a wee frothy foam;
A seemingly endless performance – it was just like the fountains of Rome.

I saw a bystander was watching; "Are you a Doctor – I need some advice?"
"A Hydrologist" came back the answer; "What you're doing is not very nice".

He said, as he looked with contempt "There is just one step you should take –
Just remove his bum from the water, before you empty the lake"!

GFF   December 1998

* * * * * * * *

15

Send for Perry Mason!

(A Speeding Offence in Nigeria)

In late February 1960 I was advised by a friend that I would shortly be receiving a summons, charging me with a speeding offence. "How do you know that?" I enquired. "Well", he informed me "I was at a dinner party attended by the Police Commissioner on Saturday and he made a point of telling everyone that *you* had overtaken his car in Aba last week and he was not very pleased"!

In due course, a police car drew into my workplace and out came a big bruiser of a police sergeant who presented me with my summons. 'You are charged with the offence of speeding, in that you drove a car in the Township of Aba at 40 mph at 7.30 am on the morning of the 3rd of February 1960 and did thus exceed the 30 mph maximum speed limit which is the allowed limit in that area'. (Or words to that effect). I was further advised that my 'case' would be heard in Enugu, the capital city of The Eastern Region, on a date in early March and that I could either attend to defend myself or I could plead guilty by letter.

"It's a fair cop." I should have said, and put pen to paper writing my crawling apology and my plea of insanity. However, my keen eyes had noticed that the date of my alleged offence was obviously incorrect – I had a perfect alibi for 3rd February, but none for the 10th which was, of course, the correct date. So, I deduced that the case would be thrown out by the court. Was I not right in assuming that, within a British Colony, justice would be dispensed as it would in 'The Old Country'?

I therefore elected to present myself in Enugu in order to defend myself. In 1960 one did not have the deep expertise we have all now gained through watching 'L A Law' and the like. However, having followed criminal justice cases on the big screen, I considered that I was fully schooled in how to represent myself.

When the charge was read out, I puffed out my chest, with super-charged confidence, and said proudly "Not guilty, your Honour". (I assumed that the man on the bench would indeed be honourable!). I had no sooner been able to start setting out my defence, saying "I was not in Aba on that day", when up popped my friend the big police sergeant to shout out "Your Honour, I have made a mistake; the date of the offence was 10th February and not the 3rd". Much to my horror, the magistrate simply said "Well, amend the date and read out the charge again." My case was in tatters!

The amended charge read "................you drove a car ....on 3rd February...........". I could hardly believe my ears – and my luck – that he had *still* got it wrong. So, once again I was able (smirking to myself) to plead "Not guilty, your Honour"! Up jumped the sergeant to stutter "I am very sorry, your Honour, I should have said *10th* February". His Honour was not a happy man and proceeded to say some rather unkind things to the poor sergeant – so much so that even I could feel a modicum of sympathy for his plight. (However, I steeled myself to be on the side of his Honour!). Now the case would surely be thrown out, as in all good films and in accordance with the full principles of British justice.

"Rewrite the charge with the correct date this time and we will see Mr. Farquhar again 4 weeks from today"! I could hardly believe my ears; surely that was not in the spirit of fair play. There was no way that I wished to return to Enugu for a further confrontation in 4 weeks' time.

Rather uncertainly I got to my feet and began to address His Lordship; "If it pleases Your Honour, I do know, from my diary, that I was in Aba on the 10th of February and I may inadvertently have slightly exceeded the speed limit on that day. If it would save the time of the court, I would be prepared to plead guilty to the Sergeant's amended charge."

His Honour got to his feet and drew himself up to what seemed, from my lowly position, like a height of over 7 feet. I knew that he knew that I had been playing a little game; I really thought he was going to jump down and strangle me, or at best, have me taken away in irons. Much to my surprise he said; "Mr. Farquhar, it is very seldom that people attending this court show the public spirit that you have just shown me. Thank you very much for being so considerate. You are admonished on this occasion. I hope I will not see you in my court again."

The Kilmacolm Literary Agency

**Thesaurus Court,
Kilmacolm, Scotland**

Professor Donald Seawright
BRISBANE

30 November, 2004

Dear Professor Seawright

'Toowoomba – Not Just a Pretty Place'

We were terribly excited to learn from our local linguistics expert Lord Farquhar of Hatfield that the above mentioned literary epic is about to explode on to bookshelves all over Australia. We want to be the first company in Scotland to offer you our congratulations and perhaps our guidance.

You are, of course, well known to us already from your earlier titles such as
   'My life with a £10 Refugee from Glasgow' and
   'Female Advocates – Why should I appeal to them?'
We love ex-lawyer writers like you and John Grisham, since you can write such good racy stories.

We can already imagine your new book becoming a best seller in the United Kingdom – assuming it can be readily translated into English. For our part, we would wish to offer to promote your book and thereafter take a large slice of your vast royalties into our coffers.

We would also like to make you aware that Britain has a Lottery Fund which has a sub-fund able to distribute money to The Arts and to 'Good Causes'. It may be that we could apply to be given some money to allow you to write a wee book about 'Kilmacolm – Not Even a Pretty Place'. Some projects, previously supported by this Fund, have proved to be even more stupid than this suggestion.

The above mentioned Lord Farquhar went on a safari to Toowoomba a few years back and has said that it really is quite a nice place, with many similarities to Kilmacolm; for example,
   The climatic conditions are identical - it rains on more than 6 days a year
   Spanish is not spoken by many of the locals
   The port and harbour areas are very small
   There are very few wild animals running around – apart from some of the residents
'Big F', as we call him, thinks that the conurbations of Toowoomba and Kilmacolm could perhaps become 'Twinned', in recognition of their commonality in having many of their present residents descended from English criminals.

When you are over in London to receive one of the many awards which will surely follow publication of your book why don't you give me a call? You could then buy me dinner whilst we discuss what I might get out of our possible association.

Yours sincerely
J Wordsworth-Smith

W A R N I N G !

THIS MACHINE IS SUBJECT TO BREAKDOWNS

DURING PERIODS OF CRITICAL NEED

A special circuit in the machine – called a **'CRITICAL DETECTOR'** – senses the operator's emotional state in terms of how desperate he or she is to use the machine and complete a task.

The Critical Detector then creates a malfunction proportional to the desperation of the operator.

Threatening the machine with violence only aggravates the situation. Likewise, any attempt to use an alternative machine will also cause it to malfunction (they belong to the same Union).

Keep cool and say nice things to the machine. Nothing else will work.

Never let anything mechanical know that you are in a hurry.

S P O G

Mrs. Fiona Price   11 July, 2002
Dumgit Cottage
DRYMEN

Dear Mrs. Price

It has come to my notice that you have taken a particular interest in Old Gits. Accordingly, I thought it might be appropriate to introduce this charitable Organisation to you in more detail.

The Society for the Protection of Old Gits (SPOG) was formed in 1952 and has done much valuable work to ensure that its members' interests are looked after. As you will be aware, many of our members are 'slightly past their prime' and they can be very sensitive. We have to guard against anyone making derogatory comments about them; so, persons suspected of Micky Taking will be pursued and legal action may result.

I should perhaps mention that we have a Sister Organisation - SPOF - which serves a similar function for Old Farts; some of their Members in Drymen or Edinburgh may be known to you. I confirm that we have no connection to societies purporting to protect birds, old B…'s and children – in fact we don't give a stuff for wild animals.

I understand that you have recently purchased some wine from our fine cellars and presented this to one of our most distinguished members. We are most grateful to you for your support. We do not qualify for Government assistance since MSPs are not really old enough to appreciate our plight (although they do often act as if they *are* senile). One of our Members did apply for Lotto money under the heading of Listed Monuments but was turned down as being beyond restoration.

As you can appreciate, we are dependent on financial support from big hearted folk like you - particularly in this our Golden Anniversary Year. Accordingly, we invite you to subscribe to our funds on a regular basis. All you have to do is to send me a cheque for £5 each month and you will be given a signed photograph of one of our Members to keep on your kitchen wall as a constant reminder of some poor Old Git.

With warmest regards

Yours sincerely

I B Smart – Hon. Secretary

Patron: The Lord Farquhar of Hatfield

MORE JOKES 1

Fencing Club Advertisement; 'New blood always welcome'.

Employee at abattoir on hearing that he is to be made redundant; "I'm just gutted".

2 elderly golfers are playing together for the first time; one with poor eyesight says; "Will you be able to follow my ball?". "Yes – my eyesight is perfect". As they walk up the fairway, after hitting good drives – "Well, where is my ball?": 2nd man says "Sorry, I can't remember".

Patient; 'I keep thinking that I am a dog'. Psychiatrist; 'Lie down on the couch and tell me all about your problem'. Patient; 'I can't do that – I'm not allowed up on a couch'.

Embarrassing situation. Visitor in a strange house had to ask her host for directions to the toilet. She could not find a light switch but, as she rather quickly closed the door, she noted the position of a bath and a sink; unable to feel for a wc, she decided just to sit on the sink. Unfortunately the sink collapsed under her weight and she hit her head on the wall. She regained consciousness to find a group of people looking at her sitting on a pile of broken plaster and porcelain – with her knickers around her ankles!

The Ravages of Time. 'An Officer was seen wearing a World War 2 uniform on a WW1 body'.

Advantage of having Alzheimer's – a) new set of friends every morning and b) no repeats on TV.

Man to Doctor; "My wife is very sensitive about her poor hearing – what can I do to assess how bad it is?" Doctor advises "Enter room and talk to her when she has her back to you; if there is no response, move slightly closer and repeat until you do get a reply." He does so with Question "What's for dinner, Dear?" He has to repeat 3 times at ever closer positions. Eventually, when almost next to her, he hears her say "For the 4th time – we're having chicken"!

Man to young boy throwing stones in the street - 'I'll have you charged'; Boy – 'You're joking'. Man – 'I'm not: I am a lawyer'; Boy – 'Honest?'. Man – 'No – just an ordinary one'!

Sign in pub: 'He who Drinketh by the Inch and Speaketh by the Yard shall be Kicketh by the Foot'

Patient; 'Doctor, I keep seeing double'. Doctor; 'Lie down on the couch and I'll examine you'. Patient; ' Which couch should I get on to?'.

Parachute fails to open as does the auxiliary 'chute. As the pilot plummets towards the ground, to his astonishment he passes a man hurtling *upwards* . He shouts across 'Excuse me, do you know anything about parachutes?' Response 'No. Do you know anything about gas cookers?'

Thatcher's Restaurant

STARTERS
Glass of Water
4 Crisps *or* a Small Handful of Nuts
1 Piece of Bread   (Butter is available as an optional extra)

FIRST COURSE
Soup of the Day   (To save you asking – it's always Veggie Broth anyway)
Warm Lettus Salad with half a Walnut and some Goats Cheese
Christmas Salmon Coulibiac   (Half normal price - to clear)
Sparrows' Heads in Aspic

COURSE SECUNDO
Fish – Served either as 'Fingers' or 'Rabbit Shapes'   (Birds quality or equal)
Steak and Kidney Gravy
Boiled Egg Slices   (2 slices per person)

TIRD COURSE
Poached Peasant with Tomato Sauce
Stuffed Italian   (Buy one, get one free)
Breast of Sparrow with a Poached Sparrow's Egg
Breadcrumbs with Steak and Kidney Gravy   (If any left from Course Secundo)
Slices of Kangaroo Beef in Australian Beer   (Can also be served without the Beef)

PUDDINGS COURSE
Toodlimisu
Custard Sauce   (Served cold or tepid)
Sticky Black Pudding with Flaming Hollandaisy Sauce

FROM THE CHEESE BOARD
Toasted Cheese   **All of our dishes are made from**
Mickyroony and Cheese   **the finest quality materials –**
                                   So is much of our food!

WINES   Choose from our Fine Selection – including
Fizzy Stuff – Dum Peregrine 1983
Shattow Laughite – 1314 (A vintage year)
Shattow Ma Fit – 2004 (ready after midnight)
Old Git – 1933

Please note that the Manageress and her Staff are all absolutely dedicated to making your visit to our Table an event to remember. If you would prefer a dish which does not appear on the above extensive and sumchus menu, please do not hesitate to bring your request to our attention.
Please also note that the Manageress reserves the right to throw out any moaners or trouble makers.

W O N D E R F L O O R S
Britain's Elite New Flooring Systems

Dr. J R Watson
Hannibal Contracts Ltd.
434 Alpine View   10 August 1985
Huddersfield

Dear Dr. Watson

As a leading expert in the design and treatment of flat roofs, we know that you will want to be kept abreast of the latest technology. Your Ph.D. Thesis "The Sponge System of Flat Roof Design" has, of course, become a standard work in this very specialist field.

During an investigation into how to stop roof leaks in many H.M. Government Establishments we discovered the secret (not that, perversely, there are many of these left in government agencies!). We invented a unique new approach. We, at WONDERFLOOR, have always believed that a positive approach to engineering problems is usually the most satisfactory. We don't simply go along with those engineers who maintain that 'if you have a hole in your roof, make a feature of it'. No – the secret is – use WONDERFLOOR Carpeting.

Apart from being water resistant,
            WONDERFLOOR is STRONG – it can span cracks up to 1 metre wide.
            WONDERFLOOR is INDESTRUCTIBLE – so, when you drop a clanger,
                             it will not be damaged.
            And, of course, when the sparks fly – it is antistatic.

Furthermore, we can offer a full range of accessories – buckets, mops, tranquilisers, etc.

SO, when your client phones you at 2am to report that his lovely new flat roof is leaking
.... DON'T PHONE THE SAMARITANS – PHONE WONDERFLOOR.............

Yours sincerely

I P Down   -   Technical Director

                    Don't forget to specify our WONDERFLOOR Central Heating

Registered UK Office: Wonder House, Legoland, Windsor QE2

23

"THE HEAT - WATCH IT"

It's 5pm and 30 C;
Lord knows what it was at ten to three:
My nose has lost a layer of skin,
My feet's on fire; my blood's gone thin.

Amawffyhot and gone tae seed;
The steam's fair rising from ma heid.
Just one thing you didn't oughter,
"Dinnae run – you'll bile your water".

G F F   1995

* * * * * * * *

GOING FOR A MAMMOGRAM

Many women are afraid of their first mammogram and, even if they have had one before, there is fear. However, there really is no need to worry since, by taking a few minutes each day, one can get reliable practice in what to expect. Each day, in the week preceding the examination, you should do a few simple practice exercises which will give a useful approximation as to what you can expect on the big day. Furthermore you can do these exercises in your own home.

EXERCISE 1
Open your refrigerator door, and insert one breast between the door and the ice box. Have one of your strongest friends slam the door as hard as possible and lean on the door for good measure. Hold that position for a full five minutes. Repeat, in case the first time was not effective.

EXERCISE 2
Visit your garage at 3 a.m. when the temperature of the concrete floor is just perfect. Take off all your clothes and lie down comfortably on your side with one breast wedged under the rear tyre of your car. Ask a friend to slowly back the car up until your breast is sufficiently flattened and chilled. Switch sides and repeat for the other breast.

EXERCISE 3
Freeze two metal bookends overnight. Strip to the waist and invite a male stranger into the room. Have this stranger press the bookends against either side of one of your breasts and smash the bookends together as hard as he is able. Ask him to call again the following day to repeat the procedure.

YOU ARE NOW PROPERLY PREPARED FOR YOUR MAMMOGRAM.

* * * * * * * *

FOOTNOTE:

Have you ever noticed how most women's problems start with men; for example;
| MENtal illness | MENtal breakdown |
| MENstrual cramps | MENopause |

Furthermore, you will probably at some time need to see a GUYnecologist and, of course, if you have serious problems you may require to have a HISterectomy.

Anon.

* * * * * * * *

2 Fairway Woods
Playa de Callaway
Costa del Big Bertha
ESPANA

Mr. A Els Kerr
Playa de Renfrew
ESCOSSE   6 August 1996

Dear Senor Kerr

I hope you not a mind that I writing this letta to you since I only lerna bout you from an olda friend in Escosse.

To introduce myself, I can say that I ave anudda very olda friend who lives in Espana – thata wonderful golfer and paella eater Severiano Ballesteros. You will not know this – since it is confidenshal – that Senor Ballesteros is gonna be the next Capitan of the Euromatics Ryder Cuppa team (Sponsor by Tetley Tee bags – my wee joke!). It is even more confidenshal that I ave beena askit by the Greata Man to be on the lookie out for hitherto unnoticed young golfing talent.

My gooda friend in Escosse – Lord Farkaros of Hatfield – he appened to mention that he had seen your name in thata great internationale newspaper, The Glasgow Eraldos, and that you, Senor Kerr, had recently won the Gaillies Open Championship, played, it was reported, under extremely difficults on one of the tufftest (or should it be 'turfless' – anudda wee joke!) courses in alla Scotlanda. Your feet has now received the widest recognition – even my Italiano pal Harry Viderchi has seen it – and as a resulta it as come to the notice of the Greata Man himself.

I should add that I met Senor Lord Farkaros when he was over in Espana on a lingustics course. He appen to notice at my golfa course that my gooda friend, Senor C Esta, had messy trousas when he arose from sleeping on a mound of grass cuttings. When he pointed this out, my pal he say "grathiass, Senor" and Lord Farkaros he say "I couldn't ave put it better myself". His Spanish is now so good as my English, and he makes a nice Spanish omelette too.

However, I digress. To return to your obvious talent, I would like to see a video of your greata feet (and perhaps a picture of your broada shoulders – anudda joke!) to pass to Senor Ballesteros. As soon as he hearda your name, Senor Kerr, he ask me to arrange that if, when he come to Troon in July, you might be available to kerry his bags up from the bus station.

I looka forward to hear from you soon.

Yoursa fatefully

A Sienda

THE OLD PENSIONERS HOSTEL
THREADBARE STREET
GLASGOW

Stewart McGrowl Esq.
Senior Partner
W A Fairhurst and Partners   20 February, 2002
GLASGOW

Dear Stewart

Thank you very much for your thoughtfulness in sending me an unstamped postcard conveying the official announcement of the Partnership's Centenary Year. May I offer you my personal congratulations?

No – not congrats on the Centenary, but on your grasp of economics. Was it Adam Smith who said 'every mickle maks a muckle'? Many Senior Partners before you have tried to find ways to cut down on expenditure, but not one was bright enough to hit upon the idea of stopping paying for stamps on mailed items. I recall an objector to the refurbishment of the office toilets when he worked out that there were to be 6 items consuming electricity (one being a heater '…which will just encourage people to sit for longer…') - compared with the amount used by the previous 1 item, a single 40 watt bulb. Again, of course, there was the classic '….it's on a time basis so give that job to staff who work very slowly…..'

As you will have read, Consignia have discovered that it costs them 42p to deal with a letter missing a 27p stamp on it. Your brilliant idea means that they can now collect 69p from pensioners like me. Don't let anyone talk *you* into Retirement before you have put more of your money saving schemes into operation!

I am returning my Postcard to you herewith. No doubt you will have the means to allow it to be cleaned up and sent on to someone else.

With kind regards

Yours – in amazement

A BRIEF INTRODUCTION TO SHAKESPEARE

Julius Caesar

Old Julius C was an N.U.T.
  A real high cockalorum.
But Brutus stabbed Old Julius C
  In the Senate near the Forum.
Mark Antonee, sarcasticlee,
  Demanded to know 'how dare he',
And Brutus died of suicide
  A sword in his chest so hairee.

Romeo and Juliet

A sweet coquet called Juliet
  To Romeo got wed, sir,
She drank a drug mixed in a mug
  And he thought that she was dead, sir.
His life he takes, and when she wakes
  She finds him dead - for certain,
She climbs on a shelf and stabs herself;
  So that brings down the curtain.

Hamlet

When Hamlet saw the Ghost, O Lor'!!
  He did get the wind up rather,
It said "I am the Bogey Man
  But once I was your father.
Now kindly kill your Uncle Bill",
  So Hamlet slew his foe, sir;
His melancholy nibs got one in the ribs
  And he kicked the bucket too, sir.

Macbeth

King Macbeth put men to death
  And found it most exciting,
Till Macduff came and stopped his game
  And the two got started fighting.
"Lay on, Macduff, for I'm hot stuff"
  Was the cry of Old Macbeth, sir,
'Til he got one on the 'Ongpompom'
  And died for the want of breath, sir.

Henry V111

King Heneree the V111, you see
  Was fond of married life, sir,
Got tired of Kate, his lawful mate,
  And took another wife, sir.
When Anne Boleyn became his queen,
  Old Wolsey came a cropper,
I could say a lot, but I'd rather not,
  For the whole thing's most improper.

Anthony and Cleopatra

A soldier free was Anthonee
  And Cleopatra lashed him;
They rode in style right up the Nile
  And there the Romans bashed him.
The knight he dies; the maid she cries
  A snake came along at night, sir;
She fell down dead upon the bed
  It served her bloody right, sir!!

Anon.

Stalag H6   Inverclyde Hospital   Puerto Greenoco

Dear Folks   31 Hulai 1985

In response to your kind enquiries about the state of my health.........I am well! Thanks for all of your Get Well cards.

I would not necessarily, until yesterday, have thought of spending my 'Fair Holiday' in this delightful fishing port (I can only assume, from the smell, that's what it is!). The experience is quite uplifting and I shall be forever grateful to my Doctor for his recommendation.

The time is only 08.15 and I have long since had breakfast and a read at the newspaper – it has been a long day so far. The night staff do not like anyone to miss the sunrise. 'Why?' I ask in my usual laconic way. Is there *snow* on the hills?' The answer today is 'Yecannyseethemfurrafog'!

I am in a very pleasant room theoretically having a view of the Firth – or there might be when the fog clears. However, because of my degenerated back, I am having to content myself with a view of the ceiling. I share a room with 3 other misfits who have orthopaedic problems, viz.

> Motor cyclist & lamppost climber – failed
> Rooftop Acrobat – failed
> Upright Wino – failed

Although the latter carries the usual local name of 'Jimmy', he speaks a language which is, if not foreign, difficult for a refined Kilmacomic to understand; eg 'A canny pit ma sair fit doon oan raflair'--------- 'Hingaboot, Jimmy'.

The staff are very attentive – so long as one remains well during their rather lengthy tea-breaks. Their looks are certainly not a distraction – I wouldn't say they are things of beauty, and I am sure even the Ugly Sisters' Recruiting Agency would reject them. This morning 'The Hangover with the Glazed Squint' got the medicines wrong again. I hadn't realised that the film 'Carry on, Nurse' was shot here!

I was delighted to hear a rumour that Prime Minister Margaret T has plans for the hospital service in Greenock. She had thoughts of selling this building; but then apparently had the brilliant idea of introducing her novel NHS economy measures instead. As a result: 1. Before I could be x-rayed yesterday, the Radiologist had to send someone out to buy a new film for the Instamatic. 2. My 40 watt lamp is fitted with a dimmer switch – the ultimate in energy saving. And 3. I was given a book to read 'Treat your own Back' – a companion volume to 'Teach yourself Surgery'.

Well, this letter was simply to re-assure you that the heavy drugs haven't had any side effects. I hope you are convinced!

Love to all......

PS: My horoscope in last night's Evening Times seemed remarkably appropriate: 'Aries – Fun trips, away days and entertainment are all there in the stars for you ....over the next 24 hours'.

A BIRTHDAY SURPRISE

A big surprise I had last month
    For Birthday number fifty;
At breakfast time my wife said nowt
    Her eyes seemed almost shifty.

My children surely would do better,
    Perhaps a little gift?;
Their memories had clearly gone,
    So I left home slightly miffed.

At work it all came right at last,
    My secretary hugged and kissed;
'Happy Birthday, Boss,' she said to me,
    The event had not been missed.

She said 'Why don't we go for lunch,
    A quiet wee meal for two';
How nice she was and she cheered me up
    That's what secretaries often do .

She booked us into a splendid place,
    The atmosphere was fine;
An intimate chat and a lovely meal
    And a glass or two of wine.

'It's such a very special day'
    She said it just like that;
'You need an afternoon of rest,
    Let's wander to my flat'.

When we arrived she said 'scuse me
    I'll change into something light;
Just make yourself at home, My Dear';
    I thought - should I not put up a fight?

"Surprise, surprise" - a party group
    Came, carrying lots of food;
My wife, my children and my friends,
    Caught me sitting - - - in the nude!!!!

GFF   2004

* * * * * * * *

MORE JOKES 2

A Texan policeman in a bar is asked why he has cut notches on the handle of his gun; 'That is to signify the number of men I have shot' he says; 'I have 10 notches for shooting bank robbers, I shot 10 murderers and 5 Mexican illegal immigrants'. 'But you have 30 notches on your gun' says an observant bystander'. 'Ah' says the policeman 'I get *bonus notches* for the Mexicans'.

'Stopping you talking is almost as difficult as stopping Readers Digest communications.'

Boatman; 'Come in number 99'. Assistant; 'But we only have 70 boats'. Boatman; 'Number 66, do you have a problem?'

Stutterer 'I've rrrrrrun iin ttto .....' Interrupter '..an old friend of mine?' Stutterer 'No, iii've rrrrrun iin ttto .....' Interrupter '..tell me the pub's on fire?' Stutterer 'No.....' Interrupter 'I haven't got all night; here's a fiver for your trouble'. Stutterer, later, to a friend 'I only wanted to tell him that I had run into his Rolls Royce'!

Energy crisis; Government announcement; 'Save energy – get cremated with a friend'

After they had gone a lot further with their lovers' play than had been intended, Mary was very pensive on the way home, before eventually saying 'Donald, if I become pregnant as a result of what we've just done, I think I'd throw myself off the mountain.' 'Oh' said Donald 'that's a big load off my mind.'

3 friends on a desert island. A genie appears and offers each man a wish. Englishman – 'I know it is Saturday, so I would like to be back in London to see Arsenal with my mates'. Whoosh – he was gone. Scotsman – 'I just wish I could join my pals in Glasgow at Parkhead'. Whoosh and he too disappeared. The Irishman then said to the genie 'I'm lonely here, I wish my 2 friends were back here with me'.......

Starter for a speech: "I'll not keep you long" – as Tony Blair said to Peter Mandelson.

The City - Statistical language 'The rate of increases in the decline of the acceleration in our profit margins is showing a marked inclination in an downward direction.'

Man talks, through a medium, to old friend who has died. On being asked what his new 'life' is like the old friend says 'A typical day starts with some sex, breakfast and then out on to the golf course; lunch, sex and out on the golf course again; I often get out on the course again after dinner and then more sex'. 'That sounds wonderful, old friend: but where are you?' 'Oh' comes the reply 'I've been changed into a rabbit at Kilmacolm Golf Course'.

Definition of 'A Mona Lisa Cocktail' - so named because 'after you've had two, you can't wipe the silly grin off your face'!

The National Health Service
Office of the Big Financial Guru

Circular to all Medical Unit Managers   October 2004

The Prime Minister has directed that, in view of his need to win over a few floating voters ahead of the proposed May General Election, an effort should be made to make all Health Service Managers appear to be more 'financially aware'. After May we can all, of course, return to our usual sloppy ways.

I have been instructed to think up a few examples of the kind of savings which might fit the bill. You may care to slip the following into the heads of your senior staff;

- Waiting lists for all procedures should never be shown to anyone
- Waiting lists can then be reduced by never adding new names
- Show gory episodes of Casualty and other hospital programmes on tv sets in waiting areas; many patients will then change their minds and go home
- Only every second patient should be given medicines, others get coloured dispirin
- Doctors and nurses can, for a bit of fun, swop uniforms - then no-one will know who is doing what. (Come to think of it, that's what we are currently like!)
- Patients in Accident and Emergency should take off their clothes in the waiting areas – to save time in the consulting units

If you wish to make any further suggestions please write directly to my Secretary; please use scraps of paper torn from medical records rather than expensive hospital stationery.

Yours faithfully

Adam Smith

SONJA SNELL

This is the tale of Sonja Snell,
To whom an accident befell.
An accident, which may seem,
Embarrassing in the extreme.
It happened, as it does to many,
That Sonja had to spend a penny.
So, off she went, with modest grace,
To the properly appointed place;

This was at the railway station,
And there she sat, in meditation.
Unfortunately, unacquainted,
The seat had been newly painted.

Poor Sonja found, to her surprise,
Her inability to rise.
She tugged, she pulled, she screamed, she yelled;
Alas, she was quite firmly held.
Her cries for help quite quickly brought
A crowd of every kind and sort,
Who stood around and laughed and sniggered –
One man said "Well, I'll be jiggered".

The stationmaster and his staff
Were most polite – they didn't laugh;
They called a carpenter at last
Who, seeing Sonja stuck quite fast,
Remarked "I know what I will do",
And promptly sawed the fixings through.
Sonja arose, only to find,
A wooden halo stuck behind.

An ambulance then came down the street;
And whipped her off, complete with seat.
They took this wooden bustle gal
Quite quickly to the hospital.

Into casualty she was led,
And laid, face downwards on a bed;
A doctor said "Upon my word,
Could anything be more absurd?

Has any one of you, I implore,
Seen such a sight as this before?"
"Yes", said a student, unashamed
"Frequently – but never framed".   Anon.

B A R R O D S

of SWEATYCOAT LANE

Dear Customer

Thank you for requesting a copy of this year's Barrods Christmas gift catalogue. I am sorry to tell you that we have not produced one this year.

We were rushed off our feet when we had our special 'off the back of a lorry' sale in October. As a result, we found ourselves with very little to advertise. It is, in our specialist business, always difficult to know what is likely to come our way at any particular time – at certain times the police are more vigilant than at others.

However, I would urge you to come along to Barrodland on any day in the week commencing 15 December. I can promise you a grotto of barrows heavily laden with the very best of almost genuine goods and some genuine authenticated copies. There will, of course, be the usual surprises – articles which have been captured from recent imports on their way to major superstores and not captured on police videos!

We urge you to take time to visit our food department in which you will find fruit and vegetables, freshly dug up during the night from the nearby allotments.

Just a word of warning – keep an eye on your wallet; if you don't you may be helping to finance next week's sale! There are some rogues around here.

I take this opportunity to wish you a very happy Christmas.

Yours sincerely

Offa Lawrie

B B C
The British Broadcasting Corporation
Office of High Quality Educational Programmes
Queen Margaret Drive   Glasgow

Hamish McData
Johnstone   Near Glasgow

1st April 1987

Dear Mr McData

Thank you for your letter of 15 March in which you asked to be considered as a contestant in the forthcoming series of 'Mastermind'.

We regret to advise you that the Board of Governors has decided that, in the present financial climate when it is difficult enough for me to afford a decent buttered scone in the BBC canteen, we are having to raise our standards. You will, of course, recall the furore raised here by the unusual specialist subject chosen recently by a shopkeeper from Glasgow : 'Anoraks – from 16 99 to 18 99 '.

Whilst we remain committed to including some contestants from the illiterate classes, you do seem to be more than usually 'educationally challenged'; we could not help but notice that you addressed your letter 'Dear Mr. Magnolia, at the Listen with Mummy Office'.

Meanwhile, we would like to thank you for your interest in our Mastermind programmes. We trust you will continue to learn something by watching either the forthcoming series or perhaps Postman Pat and The Wombles.

Yours sincerely

Magnus Magnesium
Executive Director

CITY of GLASGOW ENVIRONMENTAL STUDY

Ideas Competition

The intense interest currently being shown in creating an environmentalist's paradise in the City of Glasgow has prompted the ruling Labour Party's promotion of this exciting new competition. The first prize will be a 2 week trip, with all expenses paid, to Glasgow's glamorous River Kelvin Nature Reserve. You will, of course, have the opportunity to meet some of Glasgow's naturists in the flesh.

The Competition is open to anyone from the civilised world who can string more than two words together. Family, friends and mistresses of the Lord Provost are, however, disbarred.

All you have to do is to study the following list of possible ways to spend some the excess revenue from the Council's Housing Deficit Fund. You should then place them clearly in that order which you feel would please the Director of Roads least.

1. Pedestrianisation of the Clyde Tunnel.
2. Ornamental fountains at all city centre road junctions.
3. Replacing the City Chambers by a giant fish tank.
4. Creating a bare park within the Cathedral precincts.
5. Building a tomb for the unknown pedestrian.
6. Reducing pensions for Local Authority Highway Engineers.
7. Soft landscaping 6 lanes of the Kingston Bridge.
8. A Wind Farm at the Townhead Interchange
9. Another Competition: 'Fill in a Pothole to your own artistic design'

In the event of a tie, your completion of the following sentence (using not more than twenty five simple words) will be judged:

> *'I hate the Department of Transport because.......................'*

It is regretted that competitors cannot be allowed to add further suggestions to the above list.

A distinguished panel of experts will judge the entries. The panel includes such internationally respected celebrities as Rod Stewart, Karl Marx, Jordan and Berti Vogts.

Please post your entry – on the back of any page torn from 'A Highway Plan for Glasgow' to me....

Lord William F N Connelly
c/o The Donald Dewar Statue
Buchanan Street, Glasgow

T V Talent Spotters plc
61 The Esplanade
Bishopbriggs

7 November, 2003

Wesley Trigg Esq.
7 Flushing Meadows
Newton Mearns
GLASGOW

Dear Mr. Trigg

I am writing to say how captivated I felt when I watched your contribution to the BBC's Question Time programme last night. It was not just your verbal remarks which I noted but the whole aura which surrounded your very presence. Only very occasionally do we in the television business come across such a natural and exciting new talent, and one with such good looks – where *have* you been hiding?

As you can see from our letter heading, we are a company specialising in the selection of future stars for our screens. We would be able, for a considerable fee, to get you a placement in one of several exciting and appropriate locations.

From your attendance at Question Time you obviously have a keen interest in current affairs, and you could, therefore, be a suitable candidate to conduct the first 5 hour Cross Talk Show between Michael Howard and Tony Blair. Alternatively, your sharp mind would make you a natural as a Mastermind contestant. You might, of course, simply prefer the steady employment offered by Coronation Street or one of the other 'soaps' – in that way you would quickly, and to your benefit, gain the adulation of a large number of excitable fans.

The members of the Question Time Panel have all commented on your incisive remarks, so much so that Edwina Currie wanted to meet you in person. Unfortunately, by the time she had downed a couple of gins, you had gone. Rosie Kane and John Swinney were speechless (as befits most Members of the Scottish Parliament). It strikes me at this point that David Dimbleby himself cannot go on much longer, so I could put your name forward as an obvious replacement.

The potential to launch you on a successful new career is tremendous. All you have to do is write to me, stating your preferences and giving me some brief personal details. I shall maintain absolute confidentiality (with the exception that I already have the 'Daily Record' and the 'Oban Times' lined up and waiting for your story).

Congratulations and very best wishes,

Yours sincerely

DIRECTORS

Lord Farquhar of Hatfield (Chairman)
Sir Ivan Oldbody McSporran
I B Choosing   **Prof. Ann Itee**

38

7 Flushing Meadows

Glasgow

Lord Farquhar of Hatfield
T V Talent Spotters plc
61 The Esplanade   13 November 2003
BISHOPBRIGGS

Dear Lord Farquhar

It was a pleasure to look through my mountains of mail last Saturday and find, among the many congratulatory messages, a very complimentary letter from such a distinguished person like what you are. It really is quite amazing to think that, by exposing myself for a short time on television, the result would be accolades and amazing opportunities such as you have described. I had frankly forgotten what a good looking person I have become. I am so pleased that I taped the Question Time programme and arranged for 64 copies – it has certainly solved my Christmas present list for this year.

Your name and the style of your letter reminded me of a former Partner with Fairhurst and Partners whose mischievous sense of humour led to many an unusual office memo – I just wonder if you know him? For example, shortly after the Company produced a house journal with the title 'The Fairhurst News' he came in for some suspicion as the possible author of a spoof counter-production entitled 'Not the Fairhurst News'!

Lord Farquhar, as you will appreciate, I have much to think about in terms of the many offers that are flooding in: unfortunately, I apparently just missed out on the opportunity to compere the MTV Awards. However, I understand that the Prime Minister has me in mind for his Foreign Affairs Think Tank due to my wonderful grasp of political matters.

I would like to thank you for your fantastic letter. Perhaps in relation to the world of broadcasting I have been a slow starter but I see now that, in a short while, I can become a household name. I will let you know next month, after discussions with my new manager, if I can take up your offer of assistance.

Yours sincerely

Wes (big Handsome) Trigg

CHAMBER OF COMMERCE

In the latest ocean liner there's an object made of china,
In a dinky little cupboard by each bed;
It's a honey coloured beauty, in design both chaste and fruity,
With amusing lines of blue and green and red.

Before the war, each locker held a white repulsive shocker,
On which the letters 'P and O' offended;
But the modern sleek utensil is devoid of any stencil
You are left to *guess* for what it is intended.

Yes, the old one was unsightly and it lay unsullied nightly,
So it never really stood the acid test;
Now, from Liverpool to Sydney every patriotic kidney
Is persuaded to deliver of its best.

For this is true democracy; farewell to class hypocrisy;
The era of equality arrives;
For the richest and the poorest, in the first, saloon and tourist
Get a little splash of colour in their lives.

Though its mention is forbidden, it's a shame to keep it hidden,
The whole affair is just a hollow mockery;
We should never really rest 'til they place on Everest
This jewel of trans-oceanic crockery.

Perhaps you may be tempted, just to see it filled and emptied,
It's a natural reaction goodness knows;
But 'though there be restriction on the subject, fact or fiction,
It's not a real conviction – merely "*pose*".

Sung to the tune 'Road to the Isles'

GFF Senior   c1948

* * * * * * * *

A B C CONSULTANTS
FAX TRANSMISSION

From: The Senior Partner
To: Chief Engineer – J K Smithers   23 December 1990

Subject: M74 Motorway Contract

The following message, addressed to you, was received today at my Office. I thought that, in view of its contents, you would like to know about it before you go for your Christmas Holiday.

> "Dear John
>
> Your amazing achievements in meeting the deadlines, set by The Scottish Office, for your M74 Project have been brought to my attention by the Minister of Transport.
>
> I simply could not let 1990 end without passing on to you my personal thanks, together with those of the Ministry for Fast Tracks and of the Prime Minister. Indeed, I can tell you, in absolute confidence, that Her Majesty the Queen has been overheard to remark favourably on your efforts.
>
> There is no doubt that this great nation of ours will be for ever dependent upon engineers of your calibre. Men who follow in the footsteps of your distinguished predecessors like Telford, Brunel, Stevenson and Farquhar.
>
> Please convey my congratulations to all of your staff and, in particular, to your super efficient press secretary.
>
> With all good wishes
>
> Yours sincerely
>
>
>
> Malcolm Rifkind"

There was a short PS; 'If you could perhaps make a small donation, of say £10,000, early in January, towards the Conservative Party Election Fund for Scotland, your place in history can almost certainly be assured.'

My heartiest congratulations and best wishes for 1991. Don't forget to send out our fee invoice soon.

* * * * * * * *

THE ANCIENT HISTORY

Of

THE DISTINGUISHED SURNAME 'SMITH'

Few family names evoke as much consternation among those attempting to compile their Family Tree as that of SMITH. As any UK telephone directory will suggest, the Smiths have adopted a very dominant role in changing demographic patterns throughout the Western World. Alternatives to the common name – Smit, Schmitt, Smyth and Smut – were thought to be early derivations or corruptions but closer examination of the historical record of the Clan suggests that they have probably arisen simply through an inability to spell correctly.

The Smiths can trace their history all the way back to Biblical Times. Although surnames were not in common use in the scriptures, genealogical statistics prescribe that the fourth Apostle must have been John Smith. However, it is Claudius Maximus Smithicus who is widely acknowledged as the Clan's trendsetter. Smithicus is understood to have produced 237 off-spring, although he gained no reputation for having achieved anything else of significance in his lifetime – perhaps he set the pattern on both counts, for future generations of Smiths. "Never in the field of human procreation has so much been owed by so many to so few."

The Roman Smithici, travelled the world, as was traditional for the world's first nation of jet setters – not conquering, but procreating. A study of leading manuscripts – the Domesday Book, Parole Board Registers, American Express lists and the Roll of Poll Tax Evaders – brings the inevitable conclusion that the Smiths are everywhere.

An early, but rather biased researcher – Gene` Smith –suggested that the modern name owes its roots to Anglo Saxon times and that the name meant "a worker". However, nothing could be further from the truth! It is thought that Gene` was confused in his interpretation of names like Blacksmith, Silversmith, Locksmith and Coppersmith. It has now been shown that the Blacksmiths were part of a tribe which settled in Africa (subsequently overpowered by the great Ian White Smith of Rhodesia): the Silversmiths were simply glossy and over-ornate people (the original Yuppies): the Locksmiths were hairdressers: and the Coppersmiths were custodians of law and order.

Far from being workers, the Smiths have become well known for a singular inability to hit the headlines – probably due to their quite introverted dedication to the family. It is a matter of record that no Smith has ever been President of Russia, there has been no Pope Smith, no Smith has ever walked on the moon and, perhaps of greater significance, no Smith played for either Scotland or Brazil in the 1990 Soccer World Cup Finals.

Although more famous for what they have *not* done, there have been notable exceptions to the rule. Adam Smith, in writing his "Wealth of Nations", referred to Britain as a Nation of Shopkeepers – a Tradition subsequently followed by his namesakes in Glasgow who sell books and balls of wool. Sir William Smith extended his childhood by founding the

Boys Brigade in 1883. Joseph Smith established Mormonism, which significantly allowed polygamy, in the United States. (Unfortunately he was murdered before he could take his second wife). As every sunseeking tourist will know, there is a Smith Sound in the Arctic regions of Canada connecting Kane Bay to Baffin Bay. The smallest star in the universe was thought to have been discovered by John Galileo Smith – but he was found to have been looking through the wrong end of his telescope at the time! Among the great composers and painters – nothing. In poetry, the Reverent Sydney Smith wrote the epic words (subsequently taken up by a future British Chancellor of the Exchequer - John Smith), "Poverty is no disgrace to a man, but it is confoundedly inconvenient".

In Glasgow, where the telephone directory lists some 3000 Smiths, there have been some worthwhile contributions to cultural and other activities. Peter Hewcon Smyth (whose great grandfather could not spell) became a useful civil engineer. Minnie Margaret Smith of Stepps produced a brilliant son Gordon Farquhar. Madeleine Smith achieved notoriety as a none too clever murderer (ie she was caught!). An Elaine C. Smith and a Walter Smith became somewhat famous for their contributions to The Performing Arts in Scotland. Furthermore, the booksellers and knitting wool purveyors of Glasgow have established their own empires and thus followed in the footsteps of the great tobacco barons and shipbuilders but, unlike the rival tribe – the Browns – they never actually owned a shipyard.

Returning finally to the subject of name derivatives, it is unfortunate that a Smut is simply a small dirty object, but there is no record of Smuts living in Glasgow. Smyth could simply be an anagram of Myths – and that is really what the Clan Smith is all about. Myths, myths and more myths.

The crest of the Clan Smith is quite in keeping with all aspects of their lives – very simple. It comprises 2 crossed knitting needles in a ball of wool atop a family rocking chair. The ancient family motto is "Caveat Emptor".

Footnote

The foregoing is reproduced with the
permission and authority of the
Clan's own researcher   GFF   1988
JEANNIE ALOGY SMITH.

* * * * * * * *

MORE JOKES 3

'I hear that the President always has his finger on the button'; Secretary of State 'That would be ok if we had a President who knows which is the right button'!

To woman in street 'Mary, did you know your left breast is outside your blouse?' 'My God, I must have left ma wean on the bus.'

Batsman, having been hit hard on his private parts, jumps up and down, runs across the pitch, eyes filled with tears; he is angered to hear the appeal 'howzzatt' and the response 'out'. He runs over to the man in the white coat; 'you can't give me out for a ball like that; I appeal to you'. 'No point in appealing to me, mate' says the man in the white coat 'I'm only selling the ice cream'!

Man appears with a broken arm, cuts and abrasions; He is asked by a friend; 'could you not find a weapon to defend yourself with?' Reply 'When I was attacked, I had my hand on the man's wife's bosom; whilst it is large, heavy and ample it is really a thing of beauty and not a useful weapon!'

Starters for a speech; (a) I am here to talk to the intelligencia to give you a learned oration; I would like to start by congratulating you on your choice of speaker.
(b) Your hospitality has only been exceeded by your stupidity in inviting me.
(c) Guests at a function like this can be broken down by age and sex – you lot certainly are.

Farmer to vet; '6 months ago you gave me pills to improve the performance of my bull – can you give me more?' Vet 'I can't recall the type, can you please describe them'. Farmer 'Well they were white, about an inch long and ¼ inch thick…. and, they had a sort of peppermint flavour'!

'Cross eyed teachers' – can they really control their pupils? *and* 'Do divers with chickenpox really come up to scratch?

Culture; (a) An Irish farmer has been awarded a Nobel Prize; he has been outstanding in his own field.
(b) In Paris, when they put tables and chairs out on the pavement, it's called a 'Bistro'; in Glasgow, when tables and chairs are on the pavement, it's called a 'Warrant Sale'.'

Questions by child to Dad; 'Why are tv screens not round?' 'I don't know, Son'.
'Why is boiled water so hot?'. 'Sorry, I don't know'. 'Why do trees have leaves?'. 'Sorry, Son, I don't know the answer to that'. 'Dad, I hope you don't mind my asking all these questions?' 'No, Son, if you don't ask questions you'll never learn anything'.

Farming story; Girl 'I'm taking the cow to the bull in yonder field'. Friend 'Is that not a job for your father?' Girl 'Maybe, but I was told to try the bull first'.

THE MINISTRY of DEFENCE

Whitehall London SW1

Notification of Compulsory Enlistment   November 2002

Dear Sir

Under the Emergency Powers Act 1939 (as amended by the Defence Act 1978) you are hereby notified that you are required to place yourself on standby for possible compulsory military service in the Gulf Conflict. You may shortly be given orders to depart for Saudi Arabia, where you will join either the Third Battalion of the Queens Own Suicidal Conscripts or the Second Foot and Mouth Regiment.

Due to cutbacks in Government expenditure in recent years it will be necessary for you to provide yourself with the following equipment as soon as possible:

> Combat jacket
> Trousers (preferably khaki)
> Tin helmet
> Boots (or sturdy trainers)
> Gas mask
> Map of the Combat Zone (the Ordnance Survey 1:25000 Outdoor
>   Leisure Map of Iraq will do)
> A rifle and some ammunition
> Sun tan lotion (high factor)
> A one-way air ticket to Riyadh

If you can afford it, we would also like you to buy a tank – Messrs. Vickers Defence at Barrow are currently offering conscripts a 0% finance deal on all nearly new Y-reg. Chieftains, while stocks last.

We would like to reassure you that if anything should go wrong you will receive a free burial in a graveyard of your choice, and your widow will be entitled to the new war widows pension of £1.75 per calendar month (subject to means testing).

There may be little time for formal military training before you depart, so you are advised to hire videos of the following war films and try to pick up a few ideas as you watch: The Guns of Navarone, Kelly's Heroes, A Bridge Too Far, The Longest Day, Henry V, Blazing Saddles, The Sound of Music, etc. Alternatively, if you cannot get hold of these, any old John Wayne rubbish will do.

To mentally prepare yourself for your mission, try reading the works of Wilfred Owen or Rupert Brooke. This should give you some idea of what may be involved.

Yours faithfully
Geoffrey Hoon - Minister of Defence   **This is a Bush-Blair Joint Production**

A PARODY

'Sea Fever' by John Masefield

I must go down to the seas again, to the lonely sea and the sky,
And all I ask is a tall ship and star to steer her by,
And the wheel's kick and the wind's song and the white sails shaking,
And a grey mist on the sea's face and a grey dawn breaking.

I must go down to the seas again, for the call of the running tide
Is a wild call and a clear call that may not be denied;
And all I ask is a windy day and the white clouds flying,
And the flung spray and the blown spume, and the sea-gulls crying.

I must go down to the seas again, to the vagrant gypsy life,
To the gull's way and the whale's way where the wind's like a whetted knife;
And all I ask is a merry yarn from a laughing fellow- rover,
And a quiet sleep and a sweet dream when the long trick's over.

'April' by G F Bradby

I must go back to a vest again, to a winter vest with sleeves,
And all I ask is an honest shop where the shop-men are not thieves:
And a fair price, and a free choice, and a full stretch for dining,
And a smooth touch on the bare chest, and a smooth inner lining.

I must go back to a vest again, for that which most I dread
Is a bad cold, a head cold, and a day, or more, in bed;
And all I ask is a friend's advice, and a short time for thinking,
A soft wool, and a man's size, and a good bit for shrinking.

I must go back to a vest again, for the April winds are bleak,
And the spring's way is a cold way, and my circulation weak;
And all I ask, when the cash is paid and we leave the shop together,
Is a warm fire, and an arm chair, or a decent change in the weather.

* * * * * * *

The Hatfield Nursing Home

KILMACOLM

20 March, 2001

Dear Mrs. Price

It was kind of you to send such a lovely card addressed to your Father, on the occasion of his Birthday.

I have to agree with you that he was a '......wise and noble man, versed in the ways of the world, knowing and understanding......'. I regret that I have to use the word *was*, since he has never been the same strong person that he was before the arrival of his children. I have known him since he was a beautiful and loving youngster and then, as a scholarly and perfect gentleman, always full of fun and wise counsel. It is sad to see that handsome face now wrinkled and lined through the ravages of time and unhealthy living.

I really do think that his children took advantage of this soft, easy going man who worked his little fingers to the bone in order that his offspring should have the best of everything. I can never forgive them for putting him into an Old Folks Home just because he smelt a little funny. Many aged veterans get this way if they have been treated badly. Furthermore, it is a degenerative problem which often passes to the second child.

Since his transfer to this lovely Home in the Renfrewshire desert, I am pleased to advise you that the pungent smells to which you refer tend to be lost amongst all the other countryside odours.

Perhaps you will have the opportunity to visit the Grand Old Man in the near future. Meanwhile, thank you for your thoughtfulness – especially since, due perhaps to a middle age crisis, your genetically inherited memory lapses made you a month early with your Birthday Greetings.

Yours sincerely

R Kayik - Resident Manager

ACHTUNG

ALLES LOOKENPEEPERS

Das computermachine ist nicht fur
Gerfingerpoken und mittengrabben.
Ist easy schnappen der springenwerk,
blowenfusen und poppencorken mit
spitzensparken. Ist nicht fur
gerverken bei das dummkopfen.
Wen zei ist rubbernecken und
Sightseeren, keepen hands in das
pockets - relaxen und watch das
blinkenlights.

* * * * * * *

HOW YOU KNOW WHEN YOU ARE A SENIOR CITIZEN

You were here before the pill, frozen food, credit cards and ball point pens.
"Time Sharing" meant togetherness, not a share in a property in Spain.
You were here before panti-hose, drip dry clothes, dishwashers and electric blankets.
"Cleavage" was something the butcher had. 'Aids' was a slimming biscuit.
You preceded Batman, disposable nappies, instant coffee and pizza.
They did smoke in your day but 'grass' was for mowing and 'pot' was something to cook in.
A 'gay' person was the life and soul of the party and 'coming out' was to have fun.

If you are still not sure if you qualify as a true 'Senior Citizen' the following check list may help:

Everything aches and what doesn't ache doesn't work.
The gleam in your eye is only the sun shining on your bifocals.
You feel like the morning after but realise you have not been anywhere the night before.
You get out of breath playing cards.
The only names in your little black book begin with 'Dr.'.
Your children begin to look middle aged.
You look forward to a dull evening.
You need glasses to find glasses.
You sit in a rocking chair but can't make it rock.
Your back goes out more than you do.
Your knees buckle but your belt won't.
You put your bra on back to front and find it fits better.
Your house is too big but your medicine cupboard is too small.
You sink your teeth into a steak and they stay there.
You turn out the lights for economy – not for romance.
You have all the answers but no-one asks the right questions.
You just want to live long enough to be a problem to your kids.

Anon.

* * * * * * * *

N O T
W A N T E D

This poor old Pensioner was last seen wandering in the Australian Bush.

He was seriously over-nourished, looking lost and forlorn and was clearly not in his natural habitat. He is thought to have once been a Professional Gentleman – perhaps a used car salesman or a round the world yachtsman: friends say that, although he looks both used and round, it must be many years since anyone referred to him as a gentleman.

The Samaritans have issued a statement disclaiming that he is one of their rejects but have said that, at a pinch, they will temporarily take him in.

He says, in his Who's Who entry, that he is suave and sophisticated and once considered a career in films, having auditioned for a part in one of The James Bond movies.

He is known to have used many different names in the past, such as Captain Bligh (because of his love of the sea), John Beethoven (because of his love of music), Elvis Gordon (because of his looks), Wally Caruso (because of his broken voice) and Vee Agra (because of his special needs).

He is a master of disguises (no one in his right mind would pose, as he has done, for this picture). He often adds double chins, oversized shades, speaks with a false Australian accent and hangs old wine bottle corks to his silly hat. He is thought to have a tattoo of Lenin on his right buttock.

If you should happen to come across him do not, on any account, approach him –he can be very amorous.

Instead, CONTACT Ms. Wendy Alexander MSP, Minister for lost souls in the community

ON OVERCOMING A LACK OF CONFIDENCE

A young priest was heard by an older and wiser man to give a sermon which was full of stammering and hesitation. A note containing a word of advice – the result of years of experience – was left later for the young man; " Take some vodka with you next time – Don't worry, it will look to your congregation just like water ".

The next week's sermon was delivered with amazing confidence and fluidity and the young priest was exceedingly pleased with his performance. However, the older and wiser man felt compelled to leave another note; viz.

1   Drink your vodka in modest sips – don't gulp a tumblerful

2   There are 10 Commandments – not 8

3   There were 12 Apostles – not 14

4   The Lord was consecrated – not constipated

5   Don't refer to Jesus as The Late J. C.

6   The Crucifix is not generally known as The Big T

7   The Bible refers to   "Father, Son and Holy Ghost"- not "Dad, The Lad and The Spook"

8   Jesus provided a meal of bread and fish – not breaded fish and chips

* * * * * * * *

McDuster, Milton and McDuster

Solicitors (and Providers of Escort Services)

Chancers Lane   Milkham Drigh

Lord Farkwar of Hatfield
'The Homewrecker'   27 December 2004
KILMACOLM

Dear Lord Farkwar

Evening of Christmas – Claim by The Marchioness McGuinness

I am instrucked by my esteemit client to advise you that a very serious case of Destoktion of my Client's property has been reported.

A claim with severe financial consekwenches is being made and I am in the happy position of trying to make you squirm.

The claim relates to your falling down in my client's house in Kilmacolm and destrokting in the due process a beautiful big, very expensive and rare candel.

I am setting down my view on the money what you have to pay to The Marchioness McGuinness

Destroktion by flattenin & ecstinguishen one red candel	
	£40 plus VAT = say £80.10
Spilling of some vintage champain	$100 plus VAT = $160.97
Tromatics to Hostiss	$1000 (no VAT)
Tromatics to Hoast	$2000 (no VAT)

The grand total what you owe comes to £8000.02. As you know, my client spends her money in many currencies so, if you want to pay in Euros or Nickeragune Imprendos, that will be all right by her.

Please send the money to my office to enabel me to carve out my own whack.

Yours truly

Sue Yous

(Dictated by the Big Man and sined by me)

S I C

The Suckers Insurance Company
Bleeder Street
Manchester M1 CKY

McDuster, Milton & McDuster
Solicitors and Friends of The Downtrodden
Chancers Lane
MILKHAM DRIGH   28 December, 2004

Dear Sirs

Evening of Christmas – Claim re. Incident at 6 Hatfield Court, Kilmacolm

We refer to your communication concerning the above which was delivered to our esteemed client Lord Farquhar of Hatfield.

We have to advise you that His Lordship puts an entirely different interpretation on the events leading up to the most unfortunate accident to your Client's beloved candle. He is in no doubt that he must have been jostled and pushed – perhaps it was even an attempt at sexual harassment – before losing his balance. You have to appreciate that members of the aristocracy attend many cocktail parties in large baronial halls; they then find it difficult to adapt to small rooms such as those in a wee modern bungalow and the claustrophobic effect becomes a factor.

We would like to find a formula whereby we might settle your claim in a civilised and amicable fashion, such as by supplying a replacement wick for the said damaged candle. To claim £8000 does seem a 'Diabolical Bl.... Liberty', if I may quote the exact words of our client.

If, however, you find yourself unable to accept our generous offer we will have to put the case in the hands of His Lordship's Solicitor. The matter will be dealt with in the Delhi Office of Always, Right and Right. We do not wish to terrify you, but you will know of their reputation and will have seen their television adverts such as 'Has your Granny been injured recently in an omnibus accident?' We will, of course, need time to allow Lord Farquhar to apply for legal aid.

You will be pleased to learn, I'm sure, that his Lordship's trousers and singed wallet are making a good recovery (but we beg you and your friends not to send any more sympathy cards).

Yours faithfully

R U Sic
Founder & Managing Director

HEADS OF AYR

1. I can tell you a story
   Of footballing glory
   When I played against Rangers at Ayr;
       By the time I was through
       With the bold Boys in Blue
   Fred, their goalie, was tearing his hair.

2. Straight from the start
   We all made a dart,
   We raced down the field at some rate;
       The cross came from Ted
       And I nodded my head
   The goalkeeper dived – but too late.

3. Goal two and goal three
   Were the start of the spree,
   As I leapt to my maximum height;
       Fred's eyes filled with dread
       As I nodded my head
   To the left – and he went to the right.

4. With a beautiful dive
   By half-time it was five.
   How many more could I make?
       At the sixth, he saw red
       When I nodded my head,
   And his hands were beginning to shake.

5. I was nearly in Heaven
   With goal number seven
   Fred's career was already a gonner;
       His future was dead,
       I just nodded my head.
   Was I really the Scots' Maradonna?

6. The next one was easy
   And he looked sort of queasy
   He couldn't stand up to the flood;
       I felt sorry for Fred
       When I nodded my head
   And his dive took him into the mud.

7. The Match was all mine
   When I scored number nine,
   Just as the Ref blew his whistle;
       Fred turned sort of red
       As I nodded my head,
   As if he'd been jagged by a thistle.

8. I saw him next day
   Near the new shopping way
   Where my loved one had sent me for butter;
       I said "Hi ya, Fred"
       Then I nodded my head
   And he dived past me – into the gutter.

GFF January 1989

* * * * * * *

SELF-CERTIFICATION FORM

APPLICATION TO BE ILL

Note; this Form must be submitted at least 21 days before the date on which you wish your illness to commence.

NAME.................................. WORKS No..............................

DEPARTMENT.............................. POSITION...............................

NATURE of ILLNESS...

DATE on WHICH YOU WISH ILLNESS to COMMENCE..
(Application for Pregnancy must be submitted 12 months prior to date of delivery and accompanied by Form P43/98/A)

HAVE YOU EVER PREVIOUSLY APPLIED to SUFFER FROM THIS ILLNESS..................IF YES, GIVE DATE...

DO YOU WISH ILLNESS to be SLIGHT/SEVERE/CRIPPLING/FATAL
....

IF FATAL, DO YOU WISH THIS to be CONSIDERED A PERMANENT DISABILITY
....
(Applicants wishing to suffer a fatal illness should indicate at the foot of this form whether they wish the Board of Directors to be represented at the funeral)

DO YOU WISH to SUFFER THIS ILLNESS AT
HOME/HOSPITAL/COSTA BRAVA/FLORIDA/BOGNOR REGIS
....

DO YOU WISH YOUR ILLNESS to be CONTAGIOUS..............................

IF YES, INDICATE HOW MANY PEOPLE YOU WISH to INFECT.........

HAVE YOU EVER BEEN REFUSED PERMISSION to SUFFER FROM THIS ILLNESS BEFORE..............

IF YES, GIVE FULL DETAILS...

DO YOU WISH YOUR WIFE/HUSBAND/MISTRESS to be INFORMED OF YOUR ILLNESS IF SHE/HE SHOULD ASK THE COMPANY OF YOUR WHEREABOUTS..................

I, the undersigned, declare that to the best of my knowledge the answers given above are true and accurate.

Signed.................................. Date.............................

Note;   1. Applicants are reminded that all requests are considered on merit and that more than three applications in any one year will be considered excessive.
2. Under no circumstances will permission be given for more than one fatal illness in any three year period.
3. Diseases of an anti-social nature will not be considered.

Society for the Preservation of the Image

of Harold Wilson

As representatives of the above Society we have the distinguished duty to perpetuate the memory of the Right Honourable Harold Wilson. We feel that the erection of a statue in the grounds of the Houses of Parliament would be most fitting and we are proposing to raise the sum of £5m to cover the cost of this monument and to offset part of what he cost our Nation.

We are in some doubt as to the best position for the statue; whether to place it beside that of George Washington who never told a lie or that of Lloyd George who never told the truth. We felt that Mr. Wilson was perhaps best likened to Christopher Columbus who set off in a direction he knew not, for a place he knew not and who, when he arrived, did not know where he was and, even later, did not know where he had been.

It was Moses who said "Pick up thy shovels, bring on your asses and I will lead you to the land of plenty". 3000 years later one of Mr. Wilson's disciples, Mr. Cousins, said "Lay down thy shovels, sit on your asses and I will lead you to the land of plenty".

As you are one of the fortunate members of this great community who now inhabit our land of plenty, I humbly ask you, on behalf of our Society, to give generously.

Anon.

* * * * * * * *

MORE JOKES 4

Choice of child's name; A young native Indian father often chooses a name according to the first thing he sees after the birth; eg 'Crazy Horse', 'Little Brown Cow', etc.. A stranger in Glasgow asks 'Is that why so many of your girls are called 'Hen'?

Scots often interpret names or words differently due to their superior literary skills; eg

> Kirk Douglas = A church on the Isle of Man
> Shammy Davis Junior = A young black window cleaner
> Chou en Lai = A Chinese bed and breakfast hostelry
> Steel wool = Fibre from a hydraulic ram
> Chic or Sheikh = A bare bum in the Turkish Baths

The rather old fashioned custom of 'being engaged to be married' has been likened to getting a bicycle for Christmas and not being allowed to ride it until Easter.

Grandfather, watching a worm coming out of the ground, sees grandson pulling it out. Jokingly he says 'I'll bet you a pound you can't push it back in'. Grandson goes away, gets nail varnish with which he coats the worm; he proceeds to win his pound. Next morning, Grandfather hands over another pound where-upon the honest grandson reminds him that he had been paid the previous day. Grandfather smiles sheepishly and says 'that one's from your grandmother'!

3 animals are sharing a bed – a cow, a horse and a lamb. The cow says 'Moo've over', the horse says 'neigh bother'; the lamb falls on the floor and says 'Baa stards'!

Definition of a Bore – someone who, when you say 'Good morning; how are you?', tells you.

Language: The Spanish say 'Mañana'. In Arabic the equivalent word is 'Inshallah'. However, the Irish have no word which conveys such a sense of urgency!

A man visits a priest and confesses; 'During the War I took in a young girl and hid her in my attic - in order to save her from the Nazis who were pursuing her. However, I have to confess that I did 'take advantage of her' many times'. The old wise priest said; 'On the one hand, you probably did save her life. On the other hand, you definitely did wrong by her. On balance, I think you can be forgiven'. The man thanked the priest for his judgement and off he went. Five minutes later he was back '.....by the way, Father, do I have to tell her now that the War is over?'

A bore introduces himself at a party with the words 'I don't think I know you'. The response is brief – 'and that's an arrangement that has worked very well until now'.

'The nearest he ever got to being a sportsman was when he got Athlete's Foot'.

The only thing that stopped Bonnie Prince Charlie from going on to London was the rumour that there was a toll bridge at Derby!

A true romantic; Sometimes my man can't tell the difference between my asthma and passion.

The Plan of the Master Weaver

Our lives are but weavings
That God and we prepare;
Each life becomes a fabric planned
And fashioned in his care.
We may not always see just how
The weavings intertwine,
But we must trust the Master's hand
And follow his design.
For He can view the pattern
Upon the upper side,
While we must look from underneath
And trust in Him to guide.

Sometime a strand of sorrow
Is added to His plan;
And though it's difficult for us,
We still must understand
That it is He who fills the shuttle,
It's He who knows what's best;
So we must weave in patience
And leave to Him the rest.

Not till the loom is silent
And the shuttles cease to fly,
Shall God unroll the canvas
And explain the reason why -
The dark threads are as needed,
In the Weaver's skilful hand,
As the threads of gold and silver
In the pattern He has planned.

Anon.

c/o A B C Business Opportunities

24 November 2002

My Favourite Bank Manager
Paisley

Dear Bank Manager

I am writing to thank you for bouncing the cheque with which I endeavoured to pay my plumber last month.

By my calculations, some three nanoseconds must have elapsed between his presenting the cheque and the arrival, in my account, of the funds needed to honour it. I refer, of course, to the automatic monthly deposit of my entire salary, an arrangement which, I admit, has been in place for only eight years. You are to be commended for seizing that brief window of opportunity in order to debit my account with £50 by way of penalty.

This incident has caused me to rethink my errant financial ways. You have set me on the path of fiscal righteousness. No more will our relationship be blighted by such unpleasant incidents, since I am now restructuring my affairs in 2003 taking, as my model, the procedures, attitudes and conduct of your very own bank. I can think of no greater compliment, and I know that you will be excited and proud to hear it.

To this end, please be advised about the following changes.

In order to ensure that you have no intention of laundering the money in my Account I require you to present me with a copy of the Passport and/or Driving Licence of each of your branch employees. I also need to be shown a certified copy of the Head Office Electricity Bill for the last two years and your Chairman's entry on the Electoral Register.

I am altering my telephone system so that it reflects rather better the electronic service I receive when I try to contact you. Your nominated representative may call me at any time and will be guided through an extensive menu of options. Your employee may on occasions be put on hold but, although the wait may be lengthy if, for example, Coronation Street is on the telly, appropriate soothing music will be played. (I will try to avoid inappropriate artists with names like Sting). Please be advised that your call will possibly be important to me.

I am reviewing the charges I will be forced to pass on to you. No longer can you expect me to swallow any telephone, paper and hanging-about charges. You have been an excellent tutor and you have taught me that I should charge you for everything I can possibly think of.

May I take this opportunity of welcoming you to your new world of business opportunities with me.

Yours faithfully

THE U. K. NEWSPAPERS and Their Readers

The Financial Times   Is read by those people who run The Country

The Times   Is read by those people who think they run The Country

The Daily Mail   Is read by the wives of those who think they run The Country

The Guardian   Is read by those people who think they ought to run The Country

The Telegraph   Is read by those people who would like to run The Country

The Express   Is read by those people who used to run The Country

The Star   Is read by those who think The Country should be run by another country

The Scotsman   Is read by those people who would like Their Country not to be run by another country

The Herald   Is read by those who think Their Country should be run by Tom Shields

The Mirror   Is read by those people who don't give a stuff who runs The Country as long as she has blonde hair and big knockers

* * * * * * *

A Knowledgeable Profession

An **Architect** is said to be a man who knows a very little about a great deal and keeps knowing less and less about more and more, until he knows practically nothing about everything.

An **Engineer**, on the other hand, is a man who knows a great deal about very little and who goes along knowing more and more about less and less until finally he knows everything about nothing.

A **Contractor** starts out knowing practically everything about everything, but ends up by knowing nothing about anything

- largely due to his association with Architects and Engineers.

* * * * * * *

THE I S L A M SOCIETY

Patron :

Lord Farquhar of Hatfield

Mrs. Wean Floyd
Bridge of Weir Road
KILMACOLM

SENILITY HOUSE
50 ANDOVER TERRACE
OLDHAM

4 January 1999

Dear Mrs. Floyd

A wee sly peep at the last census has revealed your - until now - well hidden age. Please accept my congratulations on your Birthday and on your becoming quite elderly.

I know that many people become quite concerned as they pass on (if you will pardon the use of this phrase in the circumstances) from Middle Age to membership of that group known loosely as The Elderly. It was for this reason that ISLAM was founded some 80 years ago by a breakaway party from Geriatrics Anonymous. It gives me great pleasure to invite you to join our Society.

You will appreciate that the Society takes it name from the phrase "**IS** there **L**ife **A**fter **M**iddle-age", used by Sir Jonathan Creep in his original address, and not "The Institution for Sad Lumpy Adult Males" as one of our disrespectful critics has crudely described us.

Our ISLAM is not, by any means, a religious order and it is unfortunate that many people become confused and think that we are a society run by ancient Arab fanatics. Many of our Members do, of course, feel that, at this difficult period of their lives, they should seek some spiritual guidance. It is not for us, however, to point them towards Rome, Mecca or Ibrox.

The Society is here to help you. We have collected together a number of specialist publications. We hope you will find that some of those on the attached list will suit your interests.

Finally may I ask you – particularly at this time when you are just entering the prime of your old age – to spare a little something to make life a little easier for one of your less fortunate friends who is further along the geriatric path than you are. I will welcome your wee gift.

Sincerely yours

Ivan Oldbody - Secretary

THE ISLAM SOCIETY

LIST OF PUBLICATIONS

TITLE	SOURCE
"Sex for the over 50's"	Sven Goran Eriksson
"Climbing the Matterhorn"	SAGA Holidays
"Senility for Beginners"	Cliff Richards
"Sex for the under 50's"	Joan Collins
"Going for the Telegram"	Buck House Publications
"How to become Younger"	William Pitt
"Puberty – Did I miss out?"	Adrian Mole
"Teach yourself Amnesia"	?? – (we can't remember)
"D.I.Y. Undertaking"	Kerri Oot

* * * * * * * *

THE ROBIN

or A Rude Awakening

I was wakened up early one morning,
With a bird's song shrill in my ear;
A dear little robin was singing
And the sound was incredibly clear.

I could see that the dawn was just breaking
And there wasn't a cloud in the sky;
What a wonderful time to be waking
'Though I'd promised myself a long lie.

As I tip-toed over the carpet,
On the sill gleamed its body – bright red;
I took hold of the sash of the window
And I smashed it straight down on his head!

GFF   August 1983

* * * * * * *

64

THE ITALIAN WHO WENT

TO BLACKPOOL

(must be read with an Italian accent!)

One day ima go to Blackpool to a bigga Hotel. Inna morning I go down to eat soma breakfast. I tella the waitress I wanna two pissis toast. She bringa me only once piss. I tella her I wanna two piss. She say go to the toilet. I say you no understand, I wanna two piss onna my plate. She say you betta no piss onna plate, you sonna ma bitch. I don't even know the lady and she call me sonna ma bitch.

Later, I go to eat soma lunch at a bigga restaurant. The waitress she bring me a spoon ana knife, but no fock. I telle her I wanna fock. She tellsa me everyone wanna fock. I tella her, you no understand, I wanna fock on the table. She say you betta no fock on the table, you sonna ma bitch. I donna even know this lady an she calla me sonna ma bitch.

I go back to my room inna my hotel, and I see there's no shit onna my bed. I call the manager anna tella him I mussa ava shit. He tella me I should go to the toilet. I tella him, you no understand, I wanna shit onna my bed. He say you betta no shit onna bed, you sonna ma bitch.

I am very fed up, so I go to the checkout desk anna man at the desk he say 'Peace on you'. I say piss onna you too, you sonna ma bitch.

I gonna back to Italy.

Anon.

* * * * * * *

The Glasgow School of Dance

It is worth recording that there are subtle and some not so subtle differences between the techniques and styles of dance as seen in the late 20th century and those seen 50 years earlier.

Today's way of dancing is remarkably easy, and an intense study of different forms is not a pre-requisite of getting on to the floor. You simply get on to the floor, with or without a partner, and proceed to do your own thing. The noise levels are so high that you don't even have to make conversation.

Contrast this with the situation in the 1950's when everyone had to *learn* to dance. Naturally, some men were better learners than others and it was they who generally ended up with the best of the girls.

There were basically three principal methods by which one could learn:

You could make use of a sister (if you had one) who would suffer with you.
You could attend a co-educational school where dancing formed part of the curriculum.
You could go to a dance school.

I had a sister – but one who herself had two right feet – and I went to a school which was not attended by those of the fair sex. So, I had to proceed to option three. I attended, as many in Glasgow at that time did, an establishment operated by a gentleman named Roger McEwan. He and his sister Alice ran dancing schools in Sauchiehall Street. Roger was particularly renowned for his good looks and his corseted figure.

I signed up to this McEwan School of Dance for a quick course of five lessons. If one had lots of money, and ambition to really impress the 'birds', one could take ten or even twenty lessons.

I duly turned up for my first lesson, immaculately dressed, hair lightly greased (as was then the fashion), shoes gleaming and with my trousers carefully creased. I presented myself in full anticipation of the heavenly creature who was to be my instructress – that was the dream!

The reality was that I was greeted by a peely-wally fellow who directed me thus – "Plaithe your handth on my thoulders and jutht follow my thteps". Little did I know, in my ignorance of life at the time, that he led a different lifestyle from that of my own pals. I did, however, have great difficulty in controlling myself as thith creature thoftly thprayed thtructions into my ear (and spittal all down the front of my lovely shirt).

At that time there was no shortage of dance halls in Glasgow at which one could practice one's newly learned routines. They did, however, vary according to location and 'clienteele'.

Such places as the Plaza were up-market establishments where an invitation to dance would be answered with "Thenks awfully" or "No thenks, ai've denced so much already thet ai'm fair nekkered". At the Barrowland or Locarno your invitation to dance would have been answered with "Okay", or "Do you think I'm green", or the classic "Dance ma fit, China, a'm fer swettin' a'reddy". The young lady of the latter establishment, having accepted your invitation, would then 'nick her fag' and instruct her friend to keep an eye on it until her return.

The main reason for attending dances in those days was to acquire a 'lumber' – a lumber being a young lady who allowed you to take her home and snog with her for 5 minutes on her doorstep, always keeping an eye open for a protective and perhaps even outraged father.

There is the famous story told of the young man at the Locarno Ballroom who, having received permission from his dancing partner to 'see her home', asked "where do you live". "Bearsden" was the response. "Gawd" he uttered "It's a lumber I want, no' a pen pal"!

Many a romance started from those crazy dancing days; however, had it been otherwise, would we all still be single?

* * * * * * *

Ministry of Sport, Funny Walks and Counter Intelligence

The John Cleese Building
14 Funny Walk
Jim Haley Esq   **LONDON**
Captain
Kilmacolm Golf Club   Ref. SexGB/DH   21 October, 2002

Dear Mr. Haley

You may have heard that my colleagues at the FO are having a bit of bother with a Mr. Saddam Hussein - an Iraqi chappie who has developed some rather nasty weapons. The secretive blighter just won't tell us all about them. Hence, my Ministry has become involved.

Your name has been passed to me, by my good friend Lord Farquhar of Hatfield, as someone who may be able to assist us. We are particularly concerned that, amongst the weapons being developed, he has a new golf ball capable of being blasted and exploded across parts of the Middle East. (We are currently using the code word 'SexGB': *I* myself worked this out as representing 'Saddam's exploding golf ball' – smart, eh?)

His new golf ball is, we understand, not in full conformity with the Rules of the R&A - so we may have him there under Rule 5: it has pimples rather than dimples and each ball can be filled with explosives. He has also, we know, been in consultation with the Callaway Company who, unwittingly, have been developing for him a new Super Big Big Bertha with a 100 metre long shaft – this brings to mind the Supergun which was built for him in Britain in 1990.

We really do need someone like you who might put his great mind to the problem of working out a defence against this dastardly weapon. We do need a brain that has not been blunted by excessive use. In addition, we may require lateral thinking and, having heard that you do your best thinking whilst in a lateral position, we thought the post would suit you. Most importantly, we need someone with vast knowledge of the game of golf but who is, at the same time, a wee cog in an insignificant organisation. We must keep our plans secret and we hear that secrets are so well kept in Kilmacolm that no-one, including the Captain, knows what is going on. You will gather that you score highly on several counts.

If you would confirm your willingness to become involved I will report accordingly to the PM. (He is my *afternoon* boss – you see, ours is a work share department). In due course, you will, if successful, get appropriate worldwide recognition – a wee purple heart, a dacha in a country of our choice and you might perhaps even get a game for Uncle Sam's next Ryder Cup Team. For your part, you might care to send a wee minding for my department's Christmas box.

I look forward to your response.

I am, Sir, your humble and most obedient civil servant
Dick Head

Never Forget Me

Death is nothing at all: it does not count.

I have only slipped away into the next room.

Nothing has happened: everything remains exactly as it was.

I am I and you are you: and the old life that we lived so fondly
together is untouched and unchanged.

Whatever we were to each other, that we are still.

Call me by the old familiar name.

Speak of me in the easy way which you always used.

Put no difference in your tone.

Wear no forced air of solemnity or sorrow.

Laugh as we always laughed at the little jokes we enjoyed
together.

Play, smile, think of me and pray for me.

Let my name be ever the household word that it always was.

Let it be spoken without an effort, without the ghost of a
shadow upon it.

Life means all that it ever meant: it is the same as it ever was.

There is absolute and unbroken continuity.

What is this death but a negligible accident?

Why should I be out of mind because I am out of sight?

I am but waiting for you, for an interval, somewhere very near,
just around the corner.

ALL IS WELL.

Anon.

* * * * * * *

MORE JOKES 5

2 Scotsmen, having joined the Foreign Legion, are tramping through the hot arid desert, when one turns to the other; 'Do you know that today is the day of the Dunoon Highland Games, Jimmy?' Jimmy replies 'They've certainly got a great day for the Games'.

Glasgow Council definition; 'Dampness is really just a form of condensation'.

This is my second speech today. In the afternoon I got a standing ovation – from the members of Haemorrhoids Anonymous.

Schizophrenic, on LSD, was in two minds whether to jump or not.

Three Nuns ran out of petrol; having no spare supply they peed into a bottle and poured the contents into the car. A passing priest was heard to say 'I have to admire their faith'.

A nun was seen outside a pub in quite a state – shaking uncontrollably; 'I've just had an accident' she said to a passing sympathiser who offered to get her a drink to calm her nerves. 'A gin and tonic' she said 'and, because I'm a nun, please ask for it to be put in a plain cup'. On giving his order at the bar, the barman said 'Is that nun outside again'!

'To get the right answer, it helps to ask the right question'!

'Beware of the most dangerous man at a Meeting – the Articulate Incompetent'!

'Such skill, such pathos, such eloquence – such drivel!'

'His swing is to golf as Derek Jamieson's voice is to elocution'.

'I always like to start my speeches by being particularly flattering to my audience – I am, however, in your case prepared to make an exception'.

Poor memory; Fred; "where did you go for your holiday?" John; "Sorry I can't remember: but, what's that stuff that grows all over walls?" Fred; "It's ivy" John turns to his wife; "Ivy, where did we go for our holiday?"

Notice says 'Dogs must be carried on escalator'. John; "Where can I get a dog at this time of day?"

Restaurant Ad.; 'We provide absolutely anything you ask for – or we give you £100' Fred; "I'll have elephant kidneys on toast!" After a long, long wait the waiter brings over a £100 note; "Sorry, we seem to have run out of bread".

Pope John Paul was asked; "What nationality was the Good Lord Jesus – was he Polish, French, Italian?" Pope replied; "He must have been Irish: where else would you find a man of 33, single, and still living with his mother?"

DEFINITIONS

Innuendo	An Italian suppository
Vacuum	An empty space where the Pope lives
Psychiatrist	The last person you talk to before talking to yourself
Out of work	Ergonomically inactive
Grass widow	The wife of a dead vegetarian
Camay Knickers	People who steal soap
Mayonnaise	The French National Anthem
The Green Party	A group of recycled politicians
Genie	Someone who miraculously appears when a bottle's opened
Freemasons	People who build things for nothing
Provisional Ball	A dance organised by the IRA

* * * * * * * *

F   O   P   S

Senility House

Braindead Lane

O L D H A M

12 December, 2000

Mr. Wally Pantry
KILMACOLM

Dear Mr. Pantry

One of the directors of Senility International – our parent organisation – has kindly brought your name to my attention. Congratulations on your being so transparently mindless.

I understand that you have recently suffered a serious loss – your balance. It is a sad fact that the world is full of elderly men who simply fall over or indeed can't remember why they had previously been standing. However, do not be concerned, Mr. Puree, help is at hand. We at FOPS deal with accidents of all sorts every day – falling over accidents, accidents of birth, etc.

You could now, Mr. Peerie, be offered the deal of a lifetime – Membership of this prestigious Group (The Falling Over Prevention Society) could be yours at very advantageous rates. All you have to do is answer the few simple but very searching questions contained within the attached Questionnaire. (6 C's and 2 A's and you're in!)   Remember, however, that the value of your answers can go down as well as up.

Membership of FOPS will bring you an amazing range of benefits, including
      Insurance cover against stupidly falling over again
      Embarrassment insurance against being seen to stupidly fall over
      Your own very secret Pin Number
      A book on do it yourself fracture repairs
      Another Pin Number in case you forget the first one
      A lapel badge with your name and Pin Number on it
      Discounts on all leading brands of zimmers, splints and crutches
      A fully guaranteed do it yourself brain transplant kit
      A huge no claims bonus if you do not get plastered again within 12 weeks

Well, what do you have to do next, Mr. Perky? There are no long complicated forms to fill up – simply send your cheque for £187.50 to me. I will then, if I remember, send you a membership card and your very own mystery gift (provided you respond within 7 days and if I can recall where I put them).

Yours sincerely

I C Starrs

                  Patron: Lord Farquhar of Hatfield

F O P S

Membership Questionnaire

	A	**B**	**C**
Answer the following Questions	*yes*	*no*	*I can't remember*

At the time of your accident

Did you fall or were you pushed?

Had you taken alcohol within the previous 3 weeks?

Are you a Member of BUPA, SAGA, The Salvation Army?

Do you carry a Donor Card?

Have you already donated any part of your brain?

Did you provide an immediate urine sample?

Are you being sponsored by any of the following -
Titleist, Ping, Alcoholics Anonymous, Fred Perry?

And finally

Did Tony Blair approve your treatment?

Are you usually so stupid?

* * * * * * * *

2 Fairway Woods
St. Andrews

Raving Simpleton Esq.
Abacus Designs – Golf Dept.   16 March 1981
GLASGOW

Dear Mr. Simpleton

Thank you for sending, with your letter of 3 March, a winner's tie to commemorate my outstanding contribution in the 1980 Nidger Golf Trophy Event.

I regret that ill heath prevented my appearance at the recent Champagne Party and Presentation Ceremony. As you know, I was playing last month in the Idi Amin Classic – 'Da Windabeen Open' – as a result of which I caught something nasty.

I shall be proud to wear my new tie at all of this year's major international sports gatherings – The Geriatrics Olympiad, The Sportscrawler of the Year Dinner, The Kilmacolm Canoe Club Outing, Royal Askit, etc.

I note that payment of my appearance fee is still being withheld. My agent, Mr. Mark McComic, will be writing to you separately regarding this flagrant contravention of my Contract.

Nonetheless, I have 'pencilled in' the 7th of October as the date of this year's Nidger competition. I shall look forward to seeing you on that occasion - if you are selected.

With kind regards

Yours sincerely

Lord Farquhar

P.S. This year, could I please have a jacket instead of a tie?

STAFF NOTICE

The objective of each dedicated Company

Employee should be to analyse every

situation thoroughly, to anticipate all

problems prior to their occurrence, to have

answers for all of these problems, and to

move swiftly to solve them when

called upon.

* * * * * * * *

Footnote (pencilled in by an anonymous employee)

However, …………..

When you are up to your waist in alligators,

it is difficult to remind yourself that your

initial objective was to drain the swamp.

* * * * * * * *

THE MYSTERIOUS SOUNDS OF THE JUNGLE

Down in the jungle something stirred
    It wasn't a tiger, it wasn't a bird.
I was sure all the sounds of the jungle I knew
    But this one was different – I hadn't a clue.
I had to go forward, so the truth I could find
    In order to ease my inquisitive mind.

Down in the jungle something stirred
    I was cutting down branches – my machete it whirred.
Making a path to the source of the sound
    The noise getting clearer, vibrating the ground.

Down in the jungle something stirred
    Keep very quiet please, don't say a word.
We're now getting closer – I almost could see
    A clearing in sight and the great Mysteree.

Out in the clearing I could see what was stirred;
    A 3 legged pot – it was really absurd.
A large man was stirring the contents I'd sighted,
    His tribes-people round him were getting excited.
I was sure that the man was a re-penting sinner
    For beside him was a missionary, ready for dinner.

On closer inspection the cleric was seen
    To be bound hand and foot, and scrubbed very clean.
He was placed in the pot for a well chosen few
    The Reverent knew he was in quite a stew.
But as he reflected, his eyes opened wide;
    'Made in Falkirk', he noted, was inscribed on the side.

A warm glow came over as he sat in his pot,
    Consoled by the fact it was made by a Scot.

GFF   Nov. 2004

* * * * * * * *

Dr. George Jamieson
MUIRHEAD

21 October, 2003

Dear George

I hope you don't mind that I call you by your first name – we in New Labour feel closer to our people in this way.

My very dear friend Lord Farquhar of Hatfield has brought your name to my attention on account of your decision to take up trampolining at an age when many men are content to sit with their slippers on and read the Daily Mirror. I thought I should write and offer you my congratulations.

As you will know, I have always been an advocate of keeping fit and active; film of me on a bicycle was shown recently on television (although it was actually my tv double who was used on that occasion, for the obvious reasons of security and safety at work). However, I have recently been using the exercise bike which Carol, one day when she was massaging me after a shower, suggested would help my flabby tummy muscles. Boy, does that woman get my heart rate speeding up at times!

I have been promoting my latest initiative – no doubt you would have seen me at The Conference – to encourage the elderly to take up extreme sports. As long as they don't break their bloody necks I am sure it keeps them away from the NHS waiting lists. It also helps to give them something to occupy their fading brains other than thinking about drugs and sex. As you know, most of the members of my Cabinet take very little exercise; I got Alastair to take up running so that he might take some of them with him on the London Marathon and perhaps lose them somewhere in Docklands. Gordon is more interested in making babies these days, but Big John showed some useful pugilistic skills during the last election campaign. David at least takes his dog for a walk and Jack jumps on and off aeroplanes; the rest are content to be on Prosac and the Atkin's Diet.

I would like to use your wonderful talent and entrepreneurial spirit as an example to the Nation. You can expect to receive, in the near future, an invitation to come here to Downing Street for lunch and a chat; I would expect a small Honour might follow at some time.

With best wishes

Yours truly

P.S. If you could see your way to making a small donation to Party funds I will be even more grateful

The Friday Girls   30 July 1997
Kilmacolm

Dear Girls Friday

Our Ruby Wedding

What a wonderful surprise to receive the magnificent bouquet of flowers which you arranged to have sent to us on Monday. (Well, we know that you didn't actually arrange them yourselves, but you can take it that they weren't just thrown together any old how!). But, we digress!

The flowers have brought such a splash of colour to our otherwise bleak and monotonous lives in this isolated little island house in the middle of the Pacemuir Ocean.

We are so pleased that you have appreciated the strains that 40 years of sharing life with the one Partner can bring. You have cheered us up enormously.

With grateful thanks

Yours truly

Robinson and Crusoe Farquhar

I F

If you can keep your head when all about you
    Are losing theirs and blaming it on you;
If you can trust yourself when all men doubt you,
    But make allowances for their doubting too;

If you can wait and not be tired by waiting
    Or being lied about – don't deal in lies;
Or being hated – don't give way to hating;
    And yet don't look too good, nor talk too wise;

If you can dream and not make dreams your master;
    If you can think and not make thought your aim;
If you can meet with triumph and disaster
    And treat those two impostors just the same;

If you can bear to hear the truth you've spoken,
    Twisted by knaves to make a trap for fools;
Or watch the things you gave your life to, broken,
    And stoop to build 'em up with worn out tools;

If you can make one heap of all your winnings
    And risk it in one turn of pitch and toss,
And lose, and start again at your beginnings,
    And never breathe a word about your loss;

If you can force your heart and nerve and sinew
    To serve your turn long after they are gone,
And so hold on when there is nothing in you
    Except the will which says "Hold on!"

If you can walk with crowds and keep your virtue,
    Or walk with kings – nor lose the common touch;
If neither foes nor loving friends can hurt you;
    If all men count with you, but none too much;

If you can fill the unforgiving minute
    With sixty seconds' worth of distance run;
Yours is the earth and everything that's in it
    And – which is more – you'll be a man, my Son!

Rudyard Kipling

* * * * * * * *

"Willow   Trees"
4 The Esplanade
Bridge of Weir

Mrs. W Bells
The White House
KILMACOLM   5 October 1997

Dear Mrs. Bells

Wedding Bells Limited

I see, from your recent advertisement, that you can arrange absolutely everything for a Wedding. I am very excited at the prospect and would like to hear more.

My Mother, who is 86 years of age, has said that it is time that I 'took the plunge', so I have been thinking and dreaming quite a lot. I know that I deserve a spectacular and very extravagant wedding. I can just picture myself walking down the aisle in a dress made of white orgasma. I would love an off the shoulder design like one I saw modelled by Naomi Campbell – although I might require something a little larger (my day frocks are size 22).

I want lots of photographs and flowers and a large cake (I love cake !). A stretched limousine would, of course, fit the picture and I think No. 1 Devonshire Gardens would be the right place for my reception. I have few close friends so there won't be many guests (just Mummy and my Auntie Senga actually).

One of my principal requirements is that you arrange for me to be fixed up with a really nice man. I'm not so worried about his looks, as long as he has a big house and a luxury car. Please arrange to send a photograph of his car and photocopies of his insurance policies.

You have made me so happy at my prospects. Please write soon.

Yours excitedly

Jessica McSwiggan

15 October 1997

Miss Jessica McSwiggan

Dear Miss McSwiggan

We thank you for your esteemed order.

Everything is being done to find a "groom".

Do you have any particular requests regarding colour, race or creed?

Do you wish to consider someone who is vertically challenged?

Is baldness acceptable or would you prefer he wears a toupee?

Nothing will be too much trouble.

Go for it – it's now or never.

By the way, our charges are reasonable.

Even your mother will be pleased.

Lots of luck for the future.

Love is found in the strangest places.

Send us £2000 if you wish to proceed.

Sincerely yours

Mrs. W Bells

FAX TRANSMISSION

From: 'Desperate' of Tunbridge Wells
To: The V O Harley Street Clinic

Date: Too late

Subject: Vasectomy Operation

I wish to apply to have an operation to make me sterile. My reasons for doing this are numerous as, after 7 years of marriage and having 7 children, I have come to the conclusion that all forms of contraception are ineffective.

After getting married, I was told to use 'the rhythm method'. Despite trying the Samba, the Tango and the Foxtrot alternately my wife fell pregnant, and I suffered a hernia doing the Cha Cha; in addition, I always found it difficult to find a band at 4 o'clock in the morning. A doctor suggested that we use the 'safe period'. At that time we were living with my in-laws, and we often had to wait for up to 2 weeks to get the house to ourselves; needless to say, this was not much fun and it was not effective as a form of contraception.

A lady of several years' experience informed us that if we made love while breast feeding this could be a workable precaution. It's hardly as good as Newcastle Brown, but I did finish up with a clear skin, silky hair and a pregnant wife. Another old wive's tale was that, if my wife jumped up and down after intercourse, this would prevent pregnancy. We then found that, if my wife did this, she would end up - because her breasts had become enlarged by the previously tried method - with two black eyes, and she often knocked herself unconscious.

I asked a chemist about 'the sheath' and, after he demonstrated how easy it was to use, I bought a packet. When my wife fell pregnant again I was not surprised, as I failed to see how a sheath stretched over the thumb, as the chemist had shown me, can prevent babies.

My wife was later supplied with a 'coil' but, after several attempts to fit it, we realised that it was a left hand thread and my wife is definitely a right hand screw.

The 'dutch cap' was next. We were very hopeful of this, as it did not interfere with our sex at all. Alas, it did give my wife severe headaches since, although we were given the largest size available, it was still too tight across her forehead.

Finally we tried 'the pill'. At first it kept falling out; but then we realised that we must be using it wrongly; so she stated putting it between her knees – but this prevented me from getting anywhere near her. This did work for a while until one night she forgot the pill.

Please help with my problem. I know that, if my application is unsuccessful, we will have to resort to oral sex –and I fail to see how just talking about it can replace the real thing!

EVEN MORE JOKES 1

Tactless Chancellor, after goodwill meeting with some unemployed miners; "Well, it's all right for you lot but I'll have to go – I've got work to do".

Japanese gentleman in bank to exchange money is told 'The rate today is 330 yen'; Jap; 'But why so low? Last week I got 350 yen'; Teller explains 'Fluctuations'; Jap replies; 'And fluck you Americans'.

Man, seen by friend outside pub to be visibly upset, explains "The sign on the door says 'only guide dogs admitted' so I can't go in with *my* dog". Advice from friend; " Just pretend you are blind". As man orders a drink the barman notices the scruffy mutt and says "That's not a guide dog. Guide dogs are alsations or labradors". Quick as a flash the man asks; "And what kind did they give *me*?"

"Is that Kung Fu?" Answer; " No, he's only had 3 pints"!

"I've half a mind to study to become an accountant". Retort; "That's all you'll need"!

Minister of Defence; 'Am I only to be given £10 bn this year?' Thrifty Chancellor; 'Give everyone 100 quid and let them defend themselves'!

Robert Morley; "There comes a time when catering ceases to be catering and becomes rationing!"

Newspaper headlines; a) When General MacArthur returned to the Far East after discussions at the Pentagon; "General flies back to Front" b) The Pope, on arrival in New York, expressed his astonishment at the prostitutes there;"Pope's first question in New York; are there prostitutes here?" c) "Sex probe at School for the Blind. The police are groping for a lead".

Prime Minister; "Never mind; things *could* be worse". By the end of the week – they were!

Man seen begging in London Underground had a large placard stating 'I'm a Falklands victim'. On giving him a donation a passer-by got the muttered response 'Muchos gracias'!

Nasser Hussain was a very inspiring and considerate England cricket captain; he insisted on taking the next man in with him – it did save time.

A Friend asked that I try to find a long lost pal called Neilly Dunn; last known address 'London WC3'; London is a big place and I searched – London Eye, Marble Arch, Westminster, etc. One day, in need of a pee, I chanced upon a toilet sign 'WC' near Euston Station; 'That's it' I said in triumph. All cubicles occupied, I shouted out 'Are you Neilly Dunn?'; back came the response 'No, I've just started and there's no loo paper anyway'.

Young policeman talks to a young man, standing on a rooftop parapet, about his wife, children. job prospects, etc. and the lad still says he just wants to die. The policeman eventually says 'It is bloody cold out here for both of us, why don't you just go home and gas yourself?

New T V series 'All Creatures Great and Small'- starring Dolly Parton and Ronnie Corbett.

S O D O F F

Hatfield House
KILMACOLM

Mrs. Fiona A Price
Drumtog Lodge
DRYMEN

9 November 2002

Dear Fiona

The Registrar General has very kindly advised me that you have today reached your fortieth birthday. Apart from offering Congratulations I can, with great pleasure, invite you to join our special Group.

The Society of Distinguished Over Forty Farquhars is a very select body, having originally been founded by Lady Anne Farquhar after the Battle of Culloden in 1745. You will recall from your history books that it was Lady Anne who raised a small army of troops from several clans to support Bonnie Prince Charlie. Alas, history also shows that – as many of us have done since – she backed the wrong horse.

There are now a lot more Farquhars around than in 1745, so the Society has had to be sub-divided into smaller groupings. Our group was started by the distinguished Kilmacolm F's. Rather like the Order of The Thistle each branch of SODOFF can choose its own insignia; unlike the Thistlers our local emblem is in no way ostentatious; it is a sort of cross between a brand of gin and a banner.

The members meet at regular intervals, although it is difficult to get everyone together at one time – particularly since many of them can't remember what day of the week it is. However, our constitution allows for a quorum to be formed when only one member is present and this suits our chairman who fancies himself as a bit of a dictator.

In conclusion, I am sure that, in future, when someone asks you to which elite Societies you belong, it will give you very great pleasure to say simply 'SODOFF'.

With kind regards

Yours sincerely

L O Gorjus

Lord Farquhar of Hatfield - Chairman

My Faithful Old Jess

A shepherd needs a faithful friend,
And Jess is the one I've had;
She has always been a tireless lass
And her ageing makes me sad.

She could run and jump the styles
I'd whistle and off she'd go;
She'd chase the sheep into the pen,
Jess could beat Sebastian Coe.

But recently she's got quite lame,
Her legs get stiff and sore;
The sheep are running wild,
Jess can't jump fences any more.

I know it's tough at the end of the road,
She's been faithful all her life;
But now she's getting old and frail;
I need a dog to replace my wife.

GFF   2005

* * * * * * * *

MEMO

From; the Head of the Ministry for Obesity Prevention (MOP Head)

To: Super Nurse R Hustler   27 November, 2004
Inverclyde District

Dear Super Nurse Hustler

The Right Honourable John Reid has asked me to write and offer you the new position of Senior Flab Fighter in your District. We wish to seek your support for some exciting new initiatives which are designed to increase the misery of the unhealthy who cost the NHS an awful lot of money.

It is our intention to issue a series of directives through our flab fighters which, when approved by Brussels, can then be introduced nationally. John and I have been having a good old chuckle to ourselves as we have striven to find rules which can take away a lot of fun from the plebs but which won't directly affect the two of us.

A few of the rules currently on our 'wish list' would include
- Closing all fish and chip shops
- Stopping the production of all clothes above size 12
- Closing supermarket car parks so that customers will, if they want to over-eat, have to walk carrying their heavy shopping bags
- Stopping use of the Sticky Toffee Pudding Diet (NHS 97/54/97)
- Ignoring political correctness and any potential distress by openly calling obese people names such as 'Big Fatty'
- Placing exercise bicycles at all street corners and keeping registers of their use
- Removing chocolate fudge cake and the like from all menus except at private restaurants such as those in the House of Commons

We are also considering the 'usual' numbers fiddle - this time by changing vital statistics to the metric system on a 'one for one' conversion; ie a 72 inch waist will, at a stroke, become a much smaller 72cms and so on.

I hope you will make yourself available to our cause. It will be necessary for you to show an example by giving up all of your own conflicting bad eating habits. When you and your palate have had sufficient time to digest this offer please contact me at MOP Headquarters in my outhouse at Holyrood.

I am, Madam, your humble and obedient servant

Prof. E. Terol

This Is A Nanny State Directive

THEY ARRA PEOPLE

Oh, give them a Home
Where the Pensioners roam,
And they don't have to work any more;
They don't look very old
'Though they've just won the Gold,
Fifty-love is a helluva score.

Home, Home in the west,
Where the Banners have their little nest
Where there never is room
For those prophets of doom
Who say "Marriage is love's greatest test."

"Oh, give me a Scot"
Jack was giving it thought,
With a quick sideways glance at her purse;
'Twas in nineteen two nine,
When she'd had too much wine,
That she took him 'for better or worse'.

Home, Home in the west,
Where the Banners think they are the best;
Their children were four-
Who produced plenty more;
Ain't it time they all gave it a rest?

Oh, give him a comb
Or a shine to his dome
Since he must look his best every night;
But there seldom is heard
A discouraging word,
For his hardware's still working all right!

Holes, holes in his vest -
Fifty years are a strenuous test;
A new one is due
For he's turning quite blue,
'Cos it's cold, bloody cold, in the west.

Oh, give her a hat
And a ball and a bat,
Her opponents go off in a rage;
At bridge she's a wow;
We should ask ourselves "How?
Does the woman just not know her age?"

Home, Home in the west
Where the Banners have their little nest;
A Home full of joys
Love for 2 girls, 2 boys
Who acknowledge their start was the best.

GFF 1979 (In-laws' Golden wedding)

THE

W O K

43 The Esplanade
Killearn

S O C I E T Y

30 October, 2002

Solly Gunterson
Drymen

Hello Solly!

I understand that you suffer from patellae chondromalacia – a condition commonly known as dandruff on the knees. I wish, therefore, to offer Membership of our learned Society to you whereby you may have the opportunity of meeting with fellow sufferers and, through discussion, perhaps sharing experiences and finding possible ways to alleviate this most uncomfortable ailment.

The WOK Society is not, as the name might suggest, a Chinese cookery demonstration club. In fact, the letters in our title stand for 'Wobbly Old Knees' and we are the only learned body actively helping people with all manner of knee problems of which your 'P C' is only one. The Society has, in fact, been in existence since 1416, having been formed after the battle of Agincourt wherein many soldiers suffered extreme wear within the knee joints due to rubbing of their heavy and relatively inflexible armour plating.

I have been told that you intend to run over 26 miles through the streets of New York despite the danger that your legs could be in poor condition at the end of your anticipated 2 hour 30 minute jog. We can only express our sympathy that you are having to see New York by foot since you obviously cannot afford either a yellow cab or an underground ticket. We do wish you luck.

I would like to give you some free advice, from our vast experience, on ways to raise funds for your charity marathon run. May I suggest that, at your proposed Coffee Morning, you could raffle some of your old bandages and crepe supports – after all some people buy sweaty old football strips. Alternatively, we have found, in the past, that people love to take part in a sponsored knees up – the ladies can wear appropriate frilly dresses and undergarments; the men usually appear in frayed plus two's. A third gem, which would perhaps be considered 'risky' in any area other than Drymen, would be to charge, say, a fiver for each of your invited guests to massage your knees.

In order to formally introduce our Society, we have two surprises for you. Firstly, I can advise that our President, Lady Farquhar of Hatfield, has graciously agreed to attend your Coffee Morning on 12 November; and secondly, we attach our cheque for £100 as a little gift to help your Funds.

Yours sincerely

I M Bandy - Hon. Secretary

Patrons
The Marchioness of Drumbeg
The Rt. Hon. Timothy Price

8 November 2002

Hi Mr. Bandy!

At last I find a group of fellow sufferers.   It is such a relief to find that I am not alone.

I am so excited at being introduced to your Society and am full of questions, which I hope you will do your best to answer before I get carried away (I am due in hospital next week).

- I wonder if there is a weak knee weekly get together to share problems in the hobble department.
- Do any of your members have to go down stairs backwards?
- Serious looks of pain and all the straps I have to wear can be a bit of a give-away. Can you recommend a disguise system?

During my last marathon my hand was taken by an angel who said she was a dentist. She recognised my symptoms of 'dandruff on the knee' and said it seemed similar to trench mouth. Unfortunately she disappeared at the end of the race before I had a chance to thank her for her kindness and the anaesthetic sweetie.

I'm thrilled to learn that Lady Farquhar of Hatfield will be with us on the 12th and I thank you most sincerely for your valued donation.

I very much look forward to meeting you at some time. I am sure that we will have no trouble in recognising one another – I know that there will be 'something in the walk'.

Kind regards

Slowly Solly

The King's Theatre

Bath Street   Glasgow

Mrs. Eileen McDuster   14 January, 2005
KILMACOLM

Dear Eileen

Please forgive my informality in addressing you by your first name, but my good friend Lord Farquhar of Hatfield often talks of you, so I really feel I know you quite well.

I was delighted to see that you and some of your Kilmacolm neighbours were in the audience for my little Show yesterday evening. The ladies in your party certainly brightened up the front stalls, clothed so immaculately in your lovely imitation Versace sweaters. I know that some of your friends' husbands were with you but I was especially disappointed that Dr. McDuster could not be present – I could have been doing with his professional hands-on expertise for my early attack of Goose-bumps.

I am sure you would appreciate the enjoyment of a little bit of real culture in the course of your evening. I only hope, however, that the intricacies of the plot were not beyond your comprehension. I should add that the language spoken in parts of the Panto is not really designed for the posh folk of Kilmacolm, so we should perhaps have arranged for sub-title boards. You might not have understood all that complicated talk about 'Fur – Whit fur', etc. I know that, in Kilmacolm, one talks of residents wearing a 'Fur coat and nae…..bother' and that you would actually say 'Fir' which you think of as a kind of tree. You may also get confused with my pronunciation of 'Sex' which, as in Kelvinside, are thought of as bags for bringing coal in.

I hope I may see you in the audience when I next appear at The King's, with Brad Pitt, in my own production of Shakespeare's "As I like It" (or 'A Sweaty Night in Venice').

Until then,

Kind regards from me and my little Production Team

Sincerely yours

Elaine C Smith

HOUSE AUCTION

Conversion of a Church into Flats – Powlett Street, Melbourne

The Penthouse – Unit 10

17th February 2001 at 1.00pm

God's Gift – and on the 8th day, feeling well rested, God did his best work creating the Penthouse in The Cairns Memorial Church Development.

He commanded: Thou shalt have

- Three large bedrooms
- Spectacular views across East Melbourne
- Two huge living areas
- Floor to ceiling windows
- Separate dining area
- Three outdoor terraces
- Mixing granite with marble in perfect harmony
- Huge master bedroom with walk-in robes and full en-suite
- Security building with security parking for two cars

A true masterpiece of biblical proportions

Messrs. Biggin Scott, Richmond, Melbourne.

* * * * * * * *

212 Wellington Arcade
Oswaldtwistle

The Managing Director
Help Computers Limited
Slough   27 October, 2004

Dear Sir

My New Computer

I write to tell you that I have received my wonderful new computer from your Company.

However, I am unable to make it work since you have omitted to send me my little mouse-thing which, I am told, is an essential part of the whole system.

I cannot understand how a company of your standing can make such an elementary error. You must know that I do need a mouse.

It's not as if I can go down to my nearest hardware store and tell them I need a mouse. They probably have mouse traps but I am not looking for a DIY job! The manager of my local hardware store in any event does not know anything about computers and he would probably not know what I am talking about – he does not have my high I Q level.

I have to say that my new computer looks great on my desk. It is bright and shiny and, when I switch on the power, I get particularly excited. I went out to IKEA and bought a new desk and the whole outfit is just sitting there waiting to be used.

I wonder if you often forget, when you are dispatching your computers, to put all parts of the kit in the big box. I am sure other customers would be as angry as I am if you make a habit of such basic errors.

You may take it that I shall tell all of my friends what a slip-slap organisation you run. You will have to pull your socks up and become much more efficient.

Make sure that my mouse is sent to me by return.

Yours, in disgust

I B Smart

P. S. Since writing the above, I have discovered the wee mouse was at the bottom of the big box after all. May I wish you a Happy Christmas when it comes.

EVEN MORE JOKES 2

'Can you give me 10 pence to phone a friend?' 'Here's 20 pence; phone all your friends'!

Winston Churchhill and his enemies in the House of Commons
  (a) 'Big' Bessie Braddock who shouted out 'Churchhill you are drunk' to which Churchhill retorted 'Bessie Braddock-you are fat; but in the morning I'll be sobre'
  (b) MP for Northampton (Victor Paling) - attacked with the words 'Churchhill, you are a dirty dog'. This brought the response 'And the Member for Northampton should remember what dirty dogs do to palings'!

Statement of the Obvious; A dog was seen by its friend 'Why are you *standing* up to pee against that wall?' Reply 'The last time I did it against a wall the wall fell on top of me'.

Overheard at a bird sanctuary 'I find it very relaxing – I enjoy the tits and the warblers'. 'It sounds just like the House of Commons'!

Warmth – a little gift for a postman at Christmas; Lady welcomes him, invites him in, takes his coat, gives breakfast, entertains him in the bedroom and afterwards gives him a pound. The postman is overcome and asks "Why?". Lady answers "When I suggested to my husband that I give you a £10 tip, he said 'Screw the postman, give him a quid'. The breakfast was my own idea".

George Bernard Shaw sent 2 tickets to Winston Churchhill, whom he did not especially like, with a note 'Come to my Play and bring a friend – if you've got one!' Churchhill responded 'I'll wait until tomorrow's performance – if the Play is still running!'

First man; 'Back problems?' Friend; 'No, I'm just a little stiff from bowling'. Response; 'I always thought you lived in Kilmacolm'!

Harold Wilson to Doctor; 'I have a pain in my back'. Doctor; 'Mr. Wilson, it's hard to believe but you've twisted *yourself*'!

Margaret Thatcher to Doctor; 'I ate something that disagreed with me'. Doctor; 'I admire its courage'.

'He was as conspicuous as Ian Paisley at an IRA Convention'!

'He was as fast as Yasser Arafat on a bicycle riding through Newton Mearns'!

Comment re. the cross eyed javelin thrower; 'Well, at least she keeps the crowd on its toes'.

Two ladies in conversation; Lady from Edinburgh 'I once had my knickers torn off at a party in Glasgow'. Lady from Glasgow 'Knickers – *at a party?*'

Glaswegian definition; 'Time is on the wane' = 'The grandfather clock has fallen on the child'.

The British Broadcasting Corporation
Office of High Quality Educational Programmes
Queen Margaret Drive   Glasgow

S McGrowl Esq.   18 October, 2003
The Big Field
Welwyn Garden City

Dear Mr. McGrowl

I hope you will forgive my making this direct approach to you, rather than involve your Agent at this time.

I have been given the task of putting together a concert in aid of The Prince Andrew Trust for out of work civil engineers. It has come to my attention that, not only were you yourself a renowned civil engineer, but you have now taken up guitar playing - being the proud owner of a semi detached acoustic jazz guitar. I am not personally familiar with such an instrument but I have been led to understand that it makes one helluva noise.

It is on that note - if I can use that terrible pun - that I wish to enquire if there is some way I can entice a busy musician of your calibre to take a major part in our Concert.

You will, of course, know that the City of Glasgow is renowned for its culture; in fact it was chosen - from a short list of two - to be European City of Culture in 1992. (Newton Stewart was eliminated because its entry suggested it had more vultures than cultures). However, I digress....

Our Concert will in fact be part of Glasgow's Big Festival of Arts (rather crudely named 'The Big Farts' in the Daily Record). We intend to have a varied programme of novel events, such as a Ting Tong (for dyslectics), The Woodside Gospel Choir performing in the Wellington Church (known locally as 'The Big Wellie') and a special presentation of readings from the works of William F N Connelly.

You would be able to choose your own programme and artistes with whom you might feel comfortable (names like Shirley Bassey, Kylie Minogue and Madonna come easily to mind). I have looked over your cv and I have to say that one or two minor items do concern me: most importantly is your name; when I thought of the great artistes like Hank Williams and Hank Erchief, I immediately thought that Hank MacGee would suit you fine. Again, your general image would be greatly helped if you dyed your hair and had a good shave.

When you have had the opportunity to consider the rest of your commitments for 2004 perhaps you could speak with your agent and then we can discuss terms.

Yours sincerely

Jas. B Good   **Festival Patron:**
                                                      Lord Farquhar of Hatfield

Honest John McTurk

Agent to The Stars

Jas.B Good
B B C Scotland
Broadcasting House
GLASGOW

Prague   Essex

27th October 2003

Dear Mr. Good

Glasgow's Big Festival Of Arts

Following your letter of 18 October, I write on behalf of my Client Stewart McGrowl, 39th Earl of Galloway, from the mid point of our European Tour in Prague. We are currently touring his spectacular show, first created in The Isle of Dogs in 1982, "Rock Around the Dock".

His Earlship has an extremely full diary for the next 15 years, including major tours of the Colonies. He will be taking in parts of North America, The Antipodes and The Far East (and, hopefully, 'taking in' a few moneyed presenters as well!). By coincidence, he will be in Glasgow to visit the world famous Burrell Collection of ancient musical instruments in the Spring of 2005, at which time he could perhaps record a few bars for you (or just visit a few).

He has asked me to tell you that he is very impressed with the breadth of events covered by your programme; he did find it rather insensitive that you mention dyslexia since he himself has suffered from this affliction - plus halitosis, impetigo and ingrowing toenails - since puberty.

In view of his interest in all things cultural I am enclosing a copy of my latest album for Lord Farquhar personally. I know that he is rather old fashioned and is unlikely to have a DVD Player, so I am also enclosing a new needle for his gramophone to aid the sound quality.

I trust that your disappointment in not being able to secure the presence of my Client to anchor your Festival Concert will not lead to its cancellation. I will make a point of meeting you when we return from Eastern Europe in December since, if Glasgow is successful in its bid to get the 2012 Olympics, we might just be available for the Opening Ceremony.

Sincerely yours

Onya Bike
Manager   c. Lord Farquhar of Hatfield

ALL I HAVE IS YOURS

The life that I have
   Is all that I have,
And the life that I have
   Is yours.

The love that I have
   Of the life that I have
Is yours and yours and yours.

A sleep I shall have
   A rest I shall have
Yet death will be but a pause:

For the peace of my years
   In the long green grass
Will be yours and yours and yours.

'Code' Poem by Leo Marks - World War 2

S O F T

Pankhurst House
Spice-Beckham Street
Manchester

Mrs. E McDuster
The Boulevard
Kilmacolm

30 January 2000

Dear Mrs. McDuster

I am led to believe that, at a recent meeting of the Robert Burns Fan Club in Kilmacolm, you made a very valiant defence of the Feminist Movement against savage verbal abuse by some of the uncouth Fans. In recognition of your achievements, I have been asked, in my capacity as Honorary Secretary of our Organisation, to write and offer you Membership.

The Special Organisation for Feminist Techniques ('SOFT') was formed with a view to working out crafty ways to accelerate the change to a more matronly society. We have had several, and increasingly successful, achievements to date

A Prime Minister who was 80% female (and 20% rottweiler)

A sheep called Dolly which was 90% female (and 10% test tubes)

A football team in Greenock who play 100% like a bunch of lassies

It was Germaine Greer (formerly known in the Movement as Gigi) who, in her book 'The Female Uncle', advocated that women should simply assume all male titles – but we do need to be a little more subtle than that.

I have to say that we have been plagued in recent years by copy-cat organisations. The best known of these is the Trendy Union of Fashionable Females ('TUFF'). We 'Softies' often refer to these 'Tuffies' as 'Twaddlers Und Flatulent Fraudsters'. We enjoy some of the friendly rivalry but, under their new leader Ms. Emma Smesher (she comes from Kelvinside), they are getting up our noses.

I understand that you are rather small in stature (and indeed you confused some of the Burns' Fans who thought you were still sitting when you delivered your onslaught), so you would not be suitable as a sacrifice at the feet of racehorses. You do, however, seem to have a way with words, and we can see you, therefore, in the role of lecturing on language development and rhetoric (or 'witty patter' as Robert would have said).

When you have had an opportunity to consider our proposal, perhaps you could come and see us – in other words why not drop in to our SOFT Centre?

Yours sincerely

Patron; Lady Farquhar of Hatfield

I C Power

The National Health Service
Office of the Minister for Heads

November 2002

Subject: Mental Health Phone Instructions

Hello, and welcome to the mental health hotline; please listen carefully to the following menu which gives you an extensive choice of options. (You never got this under the Tories!).

If you are obsessive/compulsive: please press 1 repeatedly.

If you have a home-help: pleases ask them to press 2 for you.

If you have a multi-personality disorder: press 3,4,5 and 6.

If you are paranoid, we know who you are and what you want: please stay on the line so that we can trace your call.

If you are delusional: please press 7 and we will connect you to the mother ship.

If you are schizophrenic: listen carefully and a small voice will tell you which number to press.

If you are manic-depressive: it doesn't matter which number you press – no-one will answer.

If you are dyslexic: press 96969696969696.

If you have a nervous disorder: please fidget with the pound key until a representative comes on the line.

If you have amnesia: press 8 and state your name, address, telephone and fax numbers, date of birth, social security number and your mother's maiden name.

If you have post-traumatic stress disorder: s-l-o-w-l-y and c-a-r-e-f-u-l-l-y press 000.

If you have short term memory loss: press 9.

If you have short term memory loss: press 9. . If you have........Forget it.

If you have low self esteem: please hang up – all our operators are too busy to talk to the likes of you.

Please remember that, if it is not Tea-time, your call may be important to us.

The Rain Doctor

One always has to remember that customs in Africa are not always easily compared with those in the United Kingdom. *We* haven't yet learned the benefits of having rain doctors!

It really is necessary that the rain does what it is told! If, in Western Scotland, we would invest in the training of a few efficient rain doctors rather than weather forecasters could we then be in greater control of our destinies?

In Nigeria, appeasement of the Gods is sometimes essential but one has to be careful that things are done for the right reasons with an eye to the most advantageous results. At its most simple, one needs to decide 'do we want more rain, do we want less rain or wouldn't it be lovely to have a few days of none at all?' Naturally, there is always a conflict by the requirements of different factions and a bidding war often results; the wealthiest man or the strongest company can usually win against a less well off adversary.

My Company, African Industrial Enterprises, thought itself sufficiently important to employ its very own Rain Doctor. It has to be appreciated that the Directors, in their infinite wisdom, thought that there was good reason for this appointment since their home town of Aba is situated in the tropics; it does therefore get a substantial share of the world's rainfall – especially (of course) in 'the rainy season'!

On one my construction projects I faced a dilemma! Perhaps, in my youthfulness, I was being rather short sighted? However, I really could not see that it made economic sense to pay good money for the services of a Rain Doctor when I could see clearly that, while we were frantically trying to dig foundations, the rain kept pouring down into and flooding the holes we had just dug.

I was consequently forced, in my capacity of Engineer in Charge of Everything, to write the following rather succinct letter, on 9 July 1959, to the Company Secretary; 'As the Rain Doctor on the Aba Drainage Site is obviously not performing his duties to our material benefit, his employment should be terminated immediately'.

I did so with not a little trepidation regarding the reaction I might get. However, at least I had checked and ascertained that our Rain Man was one of the *lesser* cousins within the Family which owned the business!

Perhaps I was fortunate that, in 1959, I did not have to argue my case in front of a labour tribunal.

The Parrot House

The Kilmacolm Aviary*

Professor G. Turntable
Department of Parrot Technology
The University of North Greenock   11 January, 2005

Dear Professor Turntable

I hope you do not mind my writing to you personally but I have been told that you are one of the world's leading authorities on the behaviour of Parrot Owners.

In my case I am being driven mad by the manner in which my owner behaves towards me. He seems to think that I am stupid when *I* know that I have a Parrot IQ of 373 on the Polly scale; as you know, that makes me smarter than most humans and I am certainly 10 times more so than my Master.

I should advise you that I am from that rare breed – the Rainbow Crested Cockatoo, normally seen only in the Australian Bight – although, due to my mother having escaped from her cage one cold night, I am actually a cross between a Cockatoo and a Humming Bird. I myself stowed away at a young age on a P & O liner sailing from Adelaide to Liverpool and was then caught by my current Master as I was making my way up Speke High Street into the land of refugee freedom. I had fully intended to get a part time job as a cockle picker at Morecambe Bay.

However, I digress. Shortly after I was brought to this tropical paradise of Kilmacolm, my Master started to try and teach me English – not that he himself speaks the language very competently. He says he once had a West African Grey which he says could shriek, squawk and warble better than any other parrot in the world – what rubbish! He keeps saying "Hulloa" and "Pletty Polly" to me and expects me to entertain visitors to the Aviary by having me repeat these stupid words; I would rather use the words of grown intelligent men - like "Have a Nice Day, Sport" or "Intellectual Intercourse" and "Llanfairpwllgwyngyllgogerychwyndrobwllllantysiliogogogoch".

I first came across your name when I read, and very much enjoyed, the Paper which you presented to the International Parrot Conference in Madrid in 1996 on "Rare Behaviour Patterns in Bird Impediments and Why their Owners Exhibit Similar Eccentricities". You could have a field day, with my Master as your subject – and perhaps gain a D. Sc. in Parrot Technology.

When you have time, perhaps you could advise me: should I leave my home here and seek a well paid job in a Cockatoo Pollytechnic teaching noises to those tits and warblers who fancy life as Pollyticians?

Yours sincerely   ***Director of Aviation:**
                                             Lord Farquhar of Hatfield

Polly Styrene

Polly Styrene
c/o Lord Farquhar of Hatfield
The Parrot House
Kilmacolm

Pollypropoline Cottage

Kilmacolm

18 January 2005

My Dear Polly

Parrot Technology

Yours of the 11th is to hand - or, as we say in The Parrot Business, 'to Claw'....

I have to advise you that I lost my professorship some time ago due to an unfortunate incident in handling of a lovely bird in the Department. As I said to the judge at the time 'she did lead me on a bit, Sir'.

I am not an expert in Aussie birds, having always found them rather uncouth. My only positive experience was in helping an Oz cockatiel called Wally who was psychologically damaged; I was able to advise putting a pencil and paper in his cage since I recalled that Polly Wally doodles all the day! I also make a study of the Oz aerobics birds from Sydney on tv, but that's more for personal pleasure.

The crested cross-bred hummer is new to me. My own bird certainly 'hums'; in fact the whole house has an odour - which reminds me that I must clean out its cage, since I've had it for 8 months now.

I am so glad that you enjoyed my Paper. I wrote it in prison where, like that bloke in Alcatraz, I was allowed to keep a few budgies.

Now to your problem with your Master. He seems to exhibit all the symptoms of jealousy and it is likely that, as a child, he realised he was inferior to his parents' parrot. (Most problems nowadays are blamed by psychologists on childhood or pollygenetic influences.) Some ideas might come from carrying out a pollygraph to get at the truth. Alternatively,of course, it may be that this parrot died when your Master was at a sensitive age - a case of Pollygon earlyitis.

I really cannot help you much more but the idea of your going to a local Pollytechnic sounds good to me. It isn't cheep and it can be sqwaukward to get in but I feel sure that a Pollymath like you would probably qualifly.

Good Luck,

Yours sincerely

Turntable the Parrot Anorak

THE MARCH OF TIME

Just a line to say "I'm living"; that I'm not among the dead.
Though I'm getting more forgetful and mixed up in my head.

I've got used to my arthritis, to my denture I'm resigned;
I can cope with my bi-focals but - ye gods - I miss my mind.

Sometimes I can't remember - when I'm standing by the stair;
Am I going up for something, or have I just come down from there?

Before the fridge so often, my mind is full of doubt;
Now, did I put some food away, or come to take some out?

If it's not my turn to write, dear, I hope you won't feel sore;
I may *think* that I have written but I don't want to be a bore.

So remember, I do love you and wish that you lived near;
Now it's time to post this and to say 'goodbye, my dear'.

I stand beside the post box and my face - it sure is red;
Instead of posting this to you, I've opened it instead!

Anon.

* * * * * * *

THE JOYS OF FOREIGN TRAVEL

This is the tale of an Archers Tour,
They give you value – that's for sure.
Our Lawrence has us at his heel;
He leads – with Franco at the wheel.

Teutonic order sets the tone
To enter into the Russian Zone.
We've lots of memories to save;
What fun the border crossings gave!
The sights from the bus would make you weep -
12 border guards and a couple of sheep.

My head – it spins – it gets me down;
Another day, a different town.
Dobri uttrah: guten tag!
How many phrase books in my bag?

A night at leisure - our brains to fix;
But - 'It's luggage out at half past six'.
At comfort stops, the ladies queue -
5 kroners just to use the loo!
When it seems we're late to hit the sack,
Lawrence turns our watches back.

We close our eyes to have a ziz,
When up pops Lawrence with a quiz.
Tell me 'Who was Rudolph Hess?'
'Let me be, my brain's a mess'.

At last I board a plane for Home;
I sit relaxed – my mind can roam.
My next vacation I can plot-
But an Archers Tour – Surely not!

GFF June 2002
The Baltic Tour

* * * * * * * *

A B C Consultants Limited

Minutes of Management Committee Meeting

Present; D Tatched (Chairman)
M Borman   1st April 1975
I B Tite (Finance)
Z Z Gabor
D Livingston

1. Minutes of Previous Meeting

The Secretary apologised for a typing error in para. 3. The sentence should have read ".......Mr. Borman was asked to get staffed for......."
Otherwise the Minutes were accepted as a true record (memories have faded in any event).

2. Financial Situation

The Financial Guru stated that the latest draft accounts show that we are managing to spend as much money as we can get our hands on - always a good thing in times of high inflation when it is not worth keeping a surplus. It was nonetheless suggested that the accountant carry out a 'Cash Flew Analysis' in time for the next meeting.

The surplus produced by selling the offices to Gabor Enterprises has been distributed to the Partners' wives ahead of the M & S Sales. Negotiations to rent accommodation at cheap rates from the YWCA have started and the outlook is encouraging.

Arrangements are well in hand to lease rather than buy a new office bicycle and to claim for under-employment grants and social security benefits. Partners' wives (and some of their husbands!) are being urged to take courses at Government re-training centres.

In a spirited discussion on Pensions it was agreed that all Senior Partners would qualify for a big pension; Junior Partners would be accommodated at demi-pension rates.

It was reported that Goodwill has now been written out of our Accounts (since we seem to have fallen out with most of our major clients).

3. Major Contracts - Progress Reports

- Crowd Control at Strathclyde Region Offices; Studies are well in hand but are being hampered by the exponential growth of staff numbers and the consequent requirement to have overflow accommodation in London and Paris.
- Bearsden Sea Wall; A construction contract has been awarded to Antonine Builders.
- Kilmacolm Lighthouse; Design of the foundations for this 592m high tower is proving difficult. Furthermore, the client has objected to our suggested economy measure of using 40 watt bulbs.
- Others; Investigations into the subsidence at Downing Street and designs for the Tomintoul Motorway are being held in abeyance because of the recession.
- Work prospects in South America are starting to look more promising. Mr. Borman will be in charge and he hopes to recruit a Mr. Ronald Biggs as local manager. Mr Borman may need time off to travel to Israel and Mr. Biggs apparently has commitments to family in Australia and to business associates in Pentonville in London.

4. New Partner

It was noted that another partner, Mr. Khani Dayit, has been taken in. (Along with all of his existing clients, we hope!)

5. Staff Bonuses

It was agreed to accept the Government's new offer to pay several members of staff an extra £3.00 per week against future anticipated sickness. An approach will be made to have these payments transferred directly from The Treasury through The Post Office Gyratory System. (Z Z informed Mr. Livingston that this did not mean that these payments would go round and round in ever decreasing circles until they vanished up Mr. Healey's cash register.)

The Chairman, at this point, offered congratulations to Mr. Livingston on his recent Honorary Doctorate from Glasgow University. One staff member has already remarked that in future he will be probably be known in the office as 'Dr. Livingston, we presume'.

6. Health and Safety

In view of the structural condition of the offices it was agreed to purchase 6 pairs of steel toed sandshoes and 3 safety helmets. The requirements of the Happiness at Work Act (1974) have now been implemented and Mr. Frank Enstein has been appointed Happiness Officer.

It was agreed that, in view of recent accidents, all draughtsmen's stools should be fitted with safety belts.

7. New Clients

It was felt that more effort was needed to attract overseas work. Accordingly, Mr. Borman has accepted the invitation of a Mr. Rabin to join a mission to Israel in December.

It is hoped that we can employ more Chinese Draughtsmen in the Zanzibar office for our work in Beirut and South America. However, all such decisions will continue to be taken by our Dublin associates, Messrs. Pick & Shovel, and all overseas earnings will be transferred to our account with Bank Unter der Tafel of Zurich.

8. Equipment Requirements

Two new cups, to match the existing saucers, are required. A new toilet roll is also needed, although it is hoped to get more than one use from the present one.

Regarding a recent order for two cocktail cabinets for the London Office, the Financial Guru said that these would not be allowed by the Inland Revenue as capital Items.

No further spending on a central heating system is to be allowed. Instead, we will purchase 4 oz. of mint imperials per staff member per week. The wizardry of The Guru was applauded by Mr. Tatched who was pleased to hear that the word 'mint' in this context did not necessarily imply unused.

9. Any Other Business

The Partner for overseas affairs has stated that the minutes of all his meetings would be written in Arabic. When Mr. Borman stated that he would not then understand them, he was reminded that he often had difficulty in reading those written in English.

10. Vote of Thanks

The meeting closed with a vote of thanks to the charlady. Everyone then retired for the customary siesta before going home

* * * * * * * *

MY SISTER (AGED 65)

I recollect – when you were three –
You were big, and I was wee.

It didn't seem quite fair at first
(Although I rather liked being nursed);

But, later on – 'though you were taller,
The difference in our heights got smaller.

But you just couldn't bear to lose
So cheated, wearing high heeled shoes.

Until – supreme – I was in heaven
(I think it was in 'forty seven?).

But now I'm big, it matters nowt
(What was the blinking fuss about?)

'Cos 'though you barely reach my shoulder,
I'm still young – and you're much older!

GFF   May 1995

* * * * * * *

Society for the Protection of Mothers

The Office of Mummies

London   W14 5MU

Mrs. Shirley Ferguson
Edinburgh

1 March, 2003

Dear Mrs. Ferguson

You may have read reviews of a book by Alyce Faye Cleese and Brian Bates recently released by Arrow Books. The book has the intriguing title "How to Manage your Mother".

Your name has been passed to me as a person likely to be able to provide information which could be useful for my research project. I wish to produce a classic work in which I analyse the experiences of deep thinking people such as you. I will also use some of the less controversial aspects of the Book : in particular I wish to concentrate on thoughts provoked by the Authors' sub-title "Understanding the Most Difficult, Complicated and Fascinating Relationship in your Life".

You will note that I write under the auspices of 'Offmum' – the Government Regulator who has primary responsibility to ensure that all mums get a fair deal.

I wish you to place the following in the order most applicable to your upbringing; please note that it is not sufficient for my purposes that you simply write 'not applicable';
> My Mummy was a lazy good for nothing ....
> I am just like my Mother
> Life was ok until other children came along
> My Father was wonderful
> I am just like my Father

If, as a result of your upbringing, you feel that you have learned anything which has been useful in making you yourself a better mummy, please write to your MEP who will advise the Minister for Family Affairs in Brussels.

Thank you for your assistance.

Yours sincerely

I Ava Graus

THE ST. LUCIA GUEST HOUSE

Brisbane   Aussieland

HOUSE RULES for 2004

Due to our recent experiences in accommodating some Visitors from the United Kingdom we have had to set down certain basic Rules which we respectfully ask all of our Guests to obey.

Smoking. Do not smoke anywhere in the house. If you do wish to hasten your emphysema you may smoke at the bottom of the garden – but only if there are no snakes or spiders to be seen.

Pets. For many people their holiday wouldn't be the same without their beloved pet. So, if you are one of them and wish to come here, this holiday won't be the same! If you think of your beloved dog as part of the family, we can assure you we feel the same about our high quality carpets.

Lost Property. You leave it – we sell it.

The Neighbours. The woman who lives across the fence is a callous, gossiping witch and should not be trusted. If she happens to knock on the door, ignore her. If she tries to tell you anything about us, disregard it. She drinks like a fish and takes lots of pills; little wonder her husband had an affair with Jessie Sweatman at number 45.

Telephone. All calls will be charged at full international rates – regardless of where they are to. If you answer the phone to one of our children who is asking to borrow groceries, you can be sure they do not mean groceries and they certainly do not mean borrow.

No-go Areas. The top drawer of the dressing table in the master bedroom is locked for a reason. Should one of your children accidentally pry it open, then be assured that we had no idea what was in there and we will be as shocked and offended as you.

Green House. The plants in the green house are for our personal consumption – keep your hands off them.

The Boat. Feel free to use the dinghy. We share it with our neighbour at number 21 but please do not take it out if she is looking, since she suffers from the delusion that it belongs to *her*. Furthermore, she drinks rather a lot; so be patient – alcoholism is a terrible problem.

Departure. The old adage is true – leave it as you found it (unless you arrive after the Pattersons who are notorious slobs). Simple things we require you to do before you leave; please wipe all surfaces, vacuum carpets, re-varnish all wooden surfaces and re-wallpaper the bedrooms.

Finally. We realise that your summer holiday is a special time and we just know you will enjoy your stay at our cottage. If you have any queries or problems please don't hesitate to ask either of us. We'll be watching your every move from across the street.

Don and Helen - Proprietors

Mr. and Mrs. Helen Donald
Proprietors
The St. Lucia Guest House
BRISBANE

24 January, 2004

Dear Proprietors

House Rules

Thank you for sending a copy of your recently published House Rules.

My Wife and I will do our best to adhere to these during our next visit to your splendid Establishment. However, since you have now introduced an element of formality into your hitherto 'take it as you find us' policy, it might be as well that we let you know that we too have our own standards to maintain. The following would constitute our minimum requirements:

> Insurance; cover of at least A$2m against our catching fire, losing our marbles or inadvertently tripping over any of your threadbare carpets.
> Transport; we need a stairlift to upstairs areas (a 'two at a time' type preferred).
> Weather protection; An umbrella to be provided for night-time visits to the outside toilet.
> Home Entertainment; Sensitivity - no videos of Australian sporting triumphs to be shown.
> Language; The Strine language must not be used on notice-boards.
> Dress; Formality is required – kitchen and serving staff to wear black and white apparel.

We are also obliged to you for sending an up-to-date copy of your current Charges. In most cases we are pleased to note that these are not outrageously high – but then, we do realise that we are fortunate to belong to one of the world's great economies (or, at least, it was until our latest Chancellor took over). However, we must express surprise that you wish to charge corkage for BYO alcoholic drinks.

Lady Farquhar sends her regards

Yours sincerely

Lord Farquhar of Hatfield

Mr. WHATSISNAME

A familiar figure came in sight –
Good looking and very tall;
'Whatever is the fellow's name?'
I could not quite recall.

My memory for names, I know,
Was never very good
But age has made it much, much worse,
'Why?' – I never understood.

My friend was fast approaching me,
'Whatever is his name?'
Oh God, I can't remember;
"Hello". He said the same!

He moved to pass, I stood my ground;
Good friends can't be ignored.
I said "It's nice to meet again";
Why did he just seem bored?

"You really shouldn't keep me back,
I'm on my way to vote."
He clearly could not think *my* name,
I was rather pleased to note.

An image stirred within my mind,
My knees then turned to jelly.
It came to me – 'Our new MP';
I'd seen him on the telly!

GFF   October 2004

* * * * * * *

EVEN MORE JOKES 3

Language problems;   'I went to Athens on holiday for the food and the sights'
'Did you have the shish kebabs?'   'I certainly had – every day'
'Were you on The Acropolis?'   'I was never off it'.

'Lovely pub – I often go in for a pie, a pint and the lovely assistant's kind word'. 'What's the kind word?' 'Don't eat the pie'!

Judge; 'You get 3 months'. Prisoner; 'Easy, I can do that standing on my head'. Judge; 'That's Contempt of Court: a further 3 months to regain your normal posture'.

Prisoner throws carafe of water at Judge and just misses. Judge; '2 Years corrective training at a Young Offenders' prison – this will help you improve your aim in life'!

Pat and Mick celebrate winning £100,000 on Pools. Mick offers to buy 2 fish suppers before they look at a car showroom window. 'Would you fancy a Jaguar, Pat?' 'Yes' says Pat 'but I'm buying this time – you bought the fish suppers'.

Cecil Rhodes; 'Remember, Sir, that you are an Englishman and, as such, you have won first prize in the Lottery of Life'.

'Men are like clingfilm – transparent, but hard to remove once you get wrapped up in them'.

Judge; 'What share of the money did you get?' Prisoner; 'F… all, Your Honour.' Judge to Clerk of Court; 'What did he say?' Clerk; 'F… all, Your Honour' Judge; 'Funny I could have sworn I saw his lips move'.

Jewish Accountant on his knees every night; 'Lord, I pray that I will win the Lottery'. The Lord answers; 'Give me a chance - at least buy a ticket'.

Three children speak of their fathers' cowardliness. 1st child; 'When my dad found a cockroach in the bathroom, he sent for my mum to remove it' 2nd child; 'My mother was called to help when my father got a large worm on his spade' 3rd child; 'My dad is so afraid of the dark that, when mum went into hospital, he had to get the woman next door to sleep with him'.

Two flies are spotted making love on top of a bottle of sauce. Third fly; 'I didn't know you could get it on the HP'

Teacher, on seeing a pool of water on the classroom floor; 'Mary, Mary, why did you not put your hand up'. Mary; 'I did, Miss, but it ran through my fingers'!

A golfer hits his drive to behind a tree. He then tries to curl the ball around the tree, but his ball hits it, rebounds and then catches him full smack between the eyes. On arriving at the Pearly Gates, Peter inquires 'What are you here for?'. Response from golfer 'Two'!

A Mistaken Impression

A young couple about to be married were looking over a house in the country. After satisfying themselves that it was suitable they made their way home. During the journey the lady was very thoughtful and, when asked the reason, she said "Did you notice the WC, Bert?". Bert had not noticed any, so he wrote to the owner of the house asking where the WC was situated. The owner did not understand the meaning of WC but concluded that it must mean 'Wesleyan Church' and answered as follows:

"Dear Sir

I have pleasure in informing you that the WC is situated about 9 miles from the house and is capable of holding 250 persons. This is unfortunate for you if you are in the habit of going regularly but, no doubt you will be glad to know that many people take their lunches with them and make a day of it; others, who are less leisurely, go by car so that they can arrive just in time.

It will be of interest to you that my daughter was married in the WC. In fact, it was there that she first met her husband. I remember the marriage on account of the rush for seats; there were ten persons to a seat, usually occupied by four, so it was interesting to see the expressions on their faces. A wealthy resident of the district erected a bell over the door last week; it rings every time a member enters.

A bazaar is to be held next weekend, the proceeds from which are to help to provide plush seats, since members think this is a long felt want.

My wife and I are getting old now and are not able to go as regularly as we once did. It is six years since we last went and I can assure you, it pains us very much not to be able to go more regularly.

Yours sincerely......."

Anon.

Memo   **From: no. 2 Hatfield Court**

To: no. 5

5 June 1985

Dear Hausfunf

My thoughtless owners forgot to advise the H's who, I understand, are leaving the district that they want to accept the invitation to be present at your "House Cooling Party" on Saturday. They misled me – I thought this meant that they and others were getting a cool reception from the neighbours – otherwise I would have warned you earlier. We've also had a 'house cooling' of another sort recently when the miserable F's turned off the central heating – I can tell you it was not much fun.

I hope you don't get too much noise on Saturday – it's a worry if the F's are present. People talk so loudly, just so that their particular useless drivel can be heard above everyone else's; although, I have to say that it is quieter here now that the 3 rowdy kids have left.

However, they never leave us undisturbed, do they? My lot last week stuffed a lot of my orifices with Polyfilla (it was so undignified) and, as you know, they have kept amputating parts of me and adding others – so much so that, last year, I nearly had a nervous brickdown.

I was delighted to hear that you resisted strongly when big H tried to kick down one of your walls recently. I saw that his leg is in some sort of casing – good for you!

Don't people get up to the most ridiculous antics? "Anything goes within these four walls" – they keep saying, little knowing that our walls have eyes, ears and very sensitive feelings. I get so embarrassed at times. I can't understand them when they say that they enjoy getting plastered – my downstairs got plastered last year and it wasn't at all pleasant for me.

When I saw the advert of these Slater House Agent folk recently, I thought this meant that you were about to get a re-roofing job done – that would have been nice for you for the next cold winter. However, I now hear that their particular job is to get new owners for you. Really, just when we get used to one lot of insufferables, they're off and we've got to break in new inhabitants.

I hope you get luckier this time. Drop me a line and give me a few laughs about them in due course.

With best wishes

Yours truly

Hauszwei

WHAT IF?

If I could write a poem when all about would
        Laugh and say 'you're off your head';
If I could write a speech like Chuchhill could
        And deliver it 'where angels fear to tread'.

If I had jokes to tell that most folks knew
        But *I* could add a funny twist;
If I could revamp a wee story or two
        So *they* might think it's one they'd missed.

If I could write a book as Grisham might,
        And see my name in stores abroad;
If publishers would read, and then just write
        "We love your work - it's just the job".

If I could write music for dancing feet
        And lyrics were easy and fun;
If I could give a pop tune rhythm and beat
        So it jumped straight in at 'number one'

If I could be given a wee drop of fame;
        No money is needed nor praises extreme;
But always I wake at the end of this game,
        Reality tells me "It's just been a dream".

                            GFF   April 2005
                            (with apologies to Rudyard K.)

* * * * * * * *

C O S H

1 April 2004

MEMO: to The Marchioness McDuster

It has come to my notice that there have been strange rumblings in The Court in recent days.

It seems that the still and the wine making equipment at 'The Kingdom' (no.1) have been at full power for some time, in order, it has been reported by the King himself, to allow him and his good lady to provide fabulous hospitality on the occasion of their 40th Wedding Anniversary.

Whilst we must applaud this apparent confirmation that they *are* actually married, (some of the Serfs have been saying for some time that they have been simply 'living together'), the reputation of COSH is at risk.

On the one hand, our resident Anaesthetist at no. 4 has reported his concern that the alcoholic haze in the area will make his services redundant. Furthermore, it has been observed that the binoculars of the local Customs and Excise spy at no. 5 have recently been seen glinting in the strong sun-light.

The two nearby Court Servants Marquis McDuster and Countess Funnily are earnestly requested to be extremely vigilant and to bring their usual and considerable modifying influences to bear on the situation.

Meanwhile, I have decided to go away to far off lands rather than be seen in the area at this difficult time and perhaps have my own good reputation compromised. I shall, of course, use my marketing skills there and I will take orders for any booze which might - a most unlikely event - have proved to be surplus to requirements.

Lord Farquhar of Hatfield
Secretary to COSH

Notis to Contrakters What Want to Tender

1. The Work we want did is cleerly showed on the attached plans and speserfactions. Our Injunear whos had plenty of college, spent one hell of a lot of time when he drawed up these here plans and speserfactions. But nobody cannot think of everythink. Once your bid is in, that's it, Brother: from then on, anything wanted by our Injunear or any of his friends, or anybody else (except the Contrakter) shall be cunsidered as showed, speserfide, or emplide and shall be pervided by the Contrakter without no expense to nobudy, but hisself (meanin the contrakter).

2. If the Work is did without no extry expense to the Contrakter then the work will be tookdown and did over again until the extry expense to the Contrakter is satisfactory to our Injunear.

3. Our Injunear's plans is right as drawed. If sumthin is drawed wrong, it shall be discuvered by the Contrakter, kerectered, and did right with no extry expence to us. It won't cut no ice with us or our Injunear if you point out any mistakes our Injunear has drawed. If you do, it will be one hell of a long time before you do any more work for us or him (meanin the Injunear).

4. The Cotrakter is not sposed to make fun of our Injunear, his plans or the kind of work we're having did. If he do, it's just too bad for him (meanin the Contrakter).

5. Any Contrakter walking around the job with a smile on his face is subject to a revue of his bid.

6. If the Contrakter don't find all of our Injunear's mistakes before he bids for our job, or if the Contrakter ain't got enuff sence to know that our Injunear's goin to think up a bunch of new stuff that's going to have to be did before the job is completely did, then that's too bad for him (meanin the Contrakter).

7. The Contrakter gotta use all good stuff on this job – none of this crap from Japan.

* * * * * * * *

A B C Consultants

From: I B Stupid

To: U B Smart of Glasgow

16 November, 1982

Subject: Statistics

I have read your erudite exposition on "The Theory of Probabilities" (or, as the pessimist would say, "The Theory of Improbabilities").

I wholeheartedly agree that it is highly improbable that one can be precise about the results of a random sampling exercise, particularly when one considers the imprecision, within the wide upper and lower bounds, with which the samplers themselves are selected.

You will recall my own Doctorate Thesis in which I hypothesised around the example of a consultancy practice with about 300 members of staff of whom, in a random sampling exercise, 20% were found to be below average intelligence. Applying your own statistics, it is likely that this really means that between 5% and 50% of our engineering staff would be within the British Standard Coefficient of Thickness.

If, on the other hand, it is known from experience that over 90% of the population are pretty dim does this mean that

a)	Engineers are more intelligent than most professionals
b)	The average of an average is a very small number
c)	The interviewer himself has a low grey cell count
d)	The Directors of this company have been kidding themselves
e)	The Directors themselves are below average intelligence

?   ?   ?   ?   ?   ?   ?   ?   ?

TALENT   SPOTTERS   U.K. plc

61 The Esplanade

D W MacCertain Esq.   **BISHOPBRIGGS**
KILMACOLM

22 December 2003

Dear Mr. MacCertain

The Honours System

Our Chairman, The Lord Farquhar of Hatfield, has brought to my attention your dissatisfaction with the present Honours System which has apparently led to your have received nothing at all until now. I write to offer you my sympathy and perhaps just a little hope.

There is undoubtedly much talent in the UK which is going unrecognised. In your particular case, I know of your major contributions to competitive sport plus, of course, your untiring support of the brewing and whisky industries in Scotland.

However, I am delighted to advise you that help is at hand. As you might have seen in the press at the weekend, some 300 notable worthies have said some very unworthy things when, in the past, offers of Honours have been made to them. They include Graham Green, John Cleese, Kenneth McKellar and three corgis. There are, therefore, various medals in cupboards at Buck House waiting to find good homes; someone at our Downing Street Branch could, I'm sure, find one suitable to your chest size. Some of these medals, I need to warn you, have been gathering dust and grease, whilst others – made when a Mrs. Thatcher was in charge of our stocks - were made of plastic to save money.

In the event of your being successful, I have to ask you to undertake that you will not turn up for the presentation ceremony in a tee shirt, corduroys and green wellies. You may care to visit the dresser of a Michael Jagger who recently appeared in an immaculate ensemble, including leather jacket and trainers, in all black (his Honour was 'for services to New Zealand Rugby', I presume).

In any event, the whole System is now being overhauled. The head of the civil service has recently noticed that we no longer actually have an Empire. So, Talent Spotters has been awarded a contract to find alternative names. For example, we can reveal that Ladbrokes are currently offering odds of 4 to 1 on Kiss Blair's Elbow for the KBE and evens on the Order of the Bath becoming the Order of the Shower so that all members of the Cabinet will be eligible. As usual, a watchdog agency is being set up – Off-Hon I suppose they will call it. (I thought that one up myself!!)

If you have any ideas, please send your e-mail entry to www.gongs4us.com. A wee donation to Tony's 'Cronies in Power Fund' might also help to speed up your application.

Yours sincerely
Justin Time (nae MBE)

The Author

Gordon Farquhar was born in Scotland near to the City of Glasgow.

Although he had a classical education it was to engineering that he turned for a career and he graduated in Civil and Structural Engineering from Glasgow University and Imperial College.

He followed a very successful career, of which the last 25 years were spent as a Partner in a major Engineering Consultancy. He retired in 1992.

Apart from handling projects in the UK, his work took him to Nigeria and to several parts of The Middle East. He has continued his interest in travelling the world during his retirement.

His introduction to humour came by listening to the radio. He was, therefore, brought up on a diet of The Goon Show, Round the Horn and Hancock's Half-hour.

He has always been quick to find humour in a variety of situations – even in many aspects of his career which were meant to be taken more seriously! He has an original and tongue in cheek style of writing.

In retirement he continues to have fun – and give fun to others – with his pen and paper!

Printed in the United Kingdom
by Lightning Source UK Ltd.
107140UKS00002B/205-549

9 781845 490591